D0835463

LONDON IMMORTALS

Beau Brummell

Frontispiece

LONDON IMMORTALS

By

THEODORA BENSON

Nicolas Bentley drew the Pictures
(Others from Contemporary Sources)

LONDON
ALLAN WINGATE
12 BEAUCHAMP PLACE, S.W.3

BY THE SAME AUTHOR

NOVELS

Salad Days
Glass Houses
Which Way?
Façade
Concert Pitch
The Undertaker's Wife

WITH BETTY ASKWITH
(ILLUSTRATED BY NICOLAS BENTLEY)

Foreigners
Muddling Through
How to be Famous

TRAVEL BOOKS

The Unambitious Journey
In the East my Pleasure Lies

SHORT STORIES

Best Short Stories of Theodora Benson
The Man from the Tunnel and Other Stories

First published in 1951 by

ALLAN WINGATE (PUBLISHERS) LTD.

12 Beauchamp Place, London, S.W.3

Made and printed in Great Britain by
William Clowes and Sons, Limited, London and Beccles

Contents

List of Illustrations

DRAWINGS BY NICOLAS BENTLEY

FROM ENGRAVINGS, PAINTINGS, ETCETERA

Introduction

They lived in London; at the least some scenes of their histories were acted there. They lived; and they died, some in their beds, some in their shoes—a Tyburn saying which may stretch to cover many misadventures, at home or abroad, in or out of their senses, in good esteem, disgrace or neglect, broken, defiant or with peace at the last, often loved. They are evoked—a somewhat random process—by a street name, a plaque on a house, some stirring of association or fancy, a book from the lending library. I can only attempt to evoke those ghosts whom I come near to seeing; and though, district by district, a fairly ordered geographic process will be attempted, this must be a rag-bag book and random indeed.

Ever since I was told as a young child, truly or falsely, that Boadicea's last battle against the Romans was fought at King's Cross Railway Station, I have been aware of our predecessors thronging the streets each in his solitude. Not that Boadicea herself can readily qualify as a London ghost. She is so remote: a figure, yes, but a person, no—all the less if she be called Boudicca; while before one's teens one has abandoned any picture of the Iceni and the legions dodging locomotives. And many a more recent figure who is very real as a person has not greatly developed the poignant and flimsy talent to haunt. Spiritually, as we all know, our human nature in every head and heart is but too frail; corporeally, as Sir Arthur E. Shipley has reminded us, "even the Archbishop of Canterbury comprises 59 per cent. of water"; temperamentally, what ox of a man was ever all unruffled by grief, vexation and uncertainty? Yet many of the more or less illustrious dead may strike us as too substantial for ghosthood. I must be content to leave it so, else a mere catalogue of names would overflow the space allowed me. For that reason, too, the claims of style, folly and violence in the more or less obscure dead must often go unregarded. Lastly, for the same reason still, London itself must be severely circumscribed. There will be no exploration of Richmond, Twickenham, Chiswick, where so many charming people had charming villas. There will be no journey to Balham, where Charles Bravo died so strangely at his castellated house the Priory. After a few scattered calls east of the City limits, it is with the City, approached from the east, that my attempted tour will begin. Turning north at Temple Bar for Highgate and Hampstead, I shall circle west to Holland Park, south by Chelsea and Lambeth and back again. That central district called the West End will complete my endeavour.

I

From Deptford and Stepney to the Tower

John Evelyn (1620–1706), more prim as man and diarist than his friend Pepys, had a fine house and garden called Sayes Court south of the river in Deptford. In 1694 he removed to the family house at Wotton near Dorking, and let his Deptford estate to Admiral Benbow. It was, of course, conveniently situated for anyone interested in docks. Peter the Great, his thirst for knowledge of shipbuilding unslaked by the study of it in Holland, set out for England on 17th January 1698, rented Evelyn's house from Admiral Benbow and worked for three months as a man might work for bread in the dockyard. Unfortunately the dockyard could not enough absorb the energy of this "right nasty" inmate. Christopher Wren estimated the damage done by the Tsar to house and garden in those three months at £350.

£350 meant a great deal more than it does now. Wren, at the height of his fame, was at work on St Paul's and drawing a salary of £200 a year for it. It is true that he was modest as to money. "He is dragged up and down in a basket two or three times in a week for a paltry £200 a year," cried the Duchess of Marlborough, aghast at his trips about the scaffolding. Still, £350 was really something. Only £172 16*s* was recovered through the Tsar's secretary. A small public garden, Sayes Court Park, still marks the site of Evelyn's Deptford house and grounds where Peter the Great enjoyed morning exercise by having himself pushed through hedges and over flower-beds in a wheel-barrow.

In St Nicholas Church nearby is a tablet to Evelyn's daughter Mary, who died aged nineteen in 1685, "a beautiful young woman, endowed with shining qualities both of body and mind." Here too is a tablet to his son Richard, an infant prodigy, who died in 1658 at the age of five years and three days.

"At 2 years and a halfe old he could perfectly reade any of ye English, Latine, French, or Gothic letters, pronouncing the three first languages exactly. He had before the 5th yeare, or in that yeare, not only skill to reade most written hands, but to decline all the nouns, conjugate the verbs regular, and most of ye irregular . . . turn English into Latine, and vice versa . . . began himself to write legibly, and had a strong passion for Greeke. The number of verses he could recite was prodigious, and what he remember'd of the parts of playes, which he would also act; and when seeing a Plautus in one's hand, he asked what booke it was, and being told it was comedy, and too difficult for him, he wept for sorrow. . . . He had a wonderful disposition to mathematics, having by heart divers propositions of Euclid that were read to him in play. . . . As to his piety, astonishing were his applications of Scripture upon occasion, and his sense of God. . . . He declaimed against ye vanities of the world before he had seen any."

So wrote his father, in that famous diary, discovered in 1817 in an old clothes-basket at Wotton.

Besides all this, Richard was a pretty child, lively and charming in manner. He died in pain, anxious lest God should be offended at such frequent calling on His name for ease. Evelyn lost four others of his six sons in childhood. "Remember S[r]," wrote Jeremy Taylor of a double loss.

"your two boyes are two bright starres, and their innocence is secur'd, and you shall never heare evil of them agayne. Their state is safe, and heaven is given to them upon very easy termes; nothing but to be borne and die. It will cost you more trouble to get where they are. . . . Doe but consider what you would have suffer'd for their interest; you have suffer'd them to goe from you, to be great Princes in a strange country."

Somewhere also in the church of St Nicholas at Deptford was buried with scant regard Christopher Marlowe on 1st June 1593, as recorded in the parish register. All accounts of his death from a dagger through the brain in a Deptford tavern brawl lay the blame at his door. It is at times convenient to blame the silent dead to whom it does no added harm. Moreover, the ballad of *The Atheist's Tragedie* and the stories in Beard's *Theatre of God's Judgements*, More's *Palladio Tamia*, Sir William Vaughan's *Golden Grove, Moralized in Three Books*, had for purpose an awful warning of God's revenge on blasphemous and licentious free-thinkers.

A few days before the death in Deptford, one Richard Bame or Banes laid "a note" before Queen Elizabeth's council "contayninge the Opinion of one Christofer Marlye concernynge his damnable

Opinions and Judgment of Relygion and Scorne of God's Worde." Christopher becomes Marloe in the course of the "note", at Benet College (Corpus Christi) Cambridge he was entered as Marlin. The testimony was not upon oath; it rests upon one man's assertion, and, going off suddenly at a tangent, includes one incredible paragraph: a public and detailed statement by Marlowe of his intention and means to commit the penal offence of coining. Some of the damnable opinions, however, are not incredible, and it may well be that this Richard Bane or Bame might have made dangerous trouble for the accused man, had he lived. Marlowe himself may have made trouble for others, as it is thought by many that he had become a government spy. It is not, however, particularly disheartening to learn that Richard B. was hanged the following year on the 6th of December at Tyburn.

There is a curious redundancy in using Marlowe's death as a warning to atheists and blasphemers when he himself had written the first great dramatic attempt to depict the relations of man with what is normally the unseen. *The Tragical History of Dr Faustus* was only his second play, ragged and disjointed, containing much buffoonery attributed to other pens. Yet it is a thing of such beauty and such passion, upon a theme so gigantic, that it is scarce surprising that a poor young gentlewoman at one of Alleyn's performances "ran distracted and was never afterwards recovered."

Marlowe was one of a new species—the poor scholars, such as Nash, Peele, Kyd and Greene, mostly dissolute and reckless free-thinkers, who replaced such courtly singers as Spenser and Sidney. He was just two months older than Shakespeare, and perished at the age of twenty-nine. His *Edward II* is not inferior to Shakespeare's *Richard II*; though the last three acts are noted nonsense, the first two acts of *the Jew of Malta* rival *the Merchant of Venice*. If Shakespeare had died at the same age, of original plays we should have had only *Love's Labours Lost, The Comedy of Errors* and *Two Gentlemen of Verona*—the second mostly dispensable. Yet however Marlowe might have developed "those brave sublunary things" and that "fine madness" Michael Drayton praised, we know he could not have been a whole universe like Shakespeare.

Captain James Cook the circumnavigator (1728–1779) lived at 88 Mile End Road, Stepney. He was a self-made man, the son of a Yorkshire agricultural labourer, and he ran away to sea from a haberdasher's shop. He lived to survey the Antarctic and Antipodean coasts and to discover unknown islands in the deep Pacific. Newfoundland

and the St Lawrence knew him well; and he was clubbed and stabbed to death in sudden frenzy by natives of Hawaii. It is surely not in London that he would choose to revisit the glimpses of the moon.

John Richard Green (1837–1883), author of *A Short History of the English People* and the less known expansion of it, also lived in Stepney. For over three years he was Vicar of St Philip's Church, of which the vicarage is in Newark Street; a learned and rather humorous man with four preposterous curates.

In the 1860's, while Green laboured for God and man in Stepney, there was one street in the borough, leading towards the Tower, that together with its environs was much given to the Devil. This of course was Ratcliff Highway, now named St George Street. It was always full of drunken sailors of all nationalities armed with knives, criminals who preyed on them, and the women of both—often as dangerous as themselves. The police would only enter the Highway in pairs and that but for moral effect; they were helpless to keep order. Throughout the 'sixties it was a popular sport with the young bloods to go slumming in the rookeries of Gray's Inn Road or in the East End bars, sing-song caves and opium dens. They might find themselves welcome, as a generous source of booze and as something interesting to stare at. Or they might be furiously resented as coming insolently to stare themselves, like visitors to the Zoo. Then, whether or not a row broke out at the King of Prussia, the Prince Regent, the Blue Anchor, the Rose & Crown, or whichever of these and many more vice-haunts it might be, depended largely on prompt and skilled handling of the situation from one of the young bloods: some happy blend of boldness, *bonhomie* and officer material. Of evil repute among these places, where the entertainment offered was excess or obscenity and where ferocity was never far to seek, were the Jolly Sailors in Ship Alley and the Old Mahogany Bar in Wellclose Square off the Highway. To the anxiety of the police and of his entourage, the Prince of Wales, afterwards Edward VII, would insist on being smuggled down incognito to Mahogany Bar, where they showed naked women prize-fights.

Wellclose Square, between Cable Street and St George Street East, Stepney, is a quiet place today; with still a few rather nice but decaying houses that belonged to well-to-do sea-captains. And there is the Old Mahogany Bar. But if the young Edward, Queen Victoria's eldest son, should haunt it, it will offer nothing to console him for his strict Prussian upbringing: "the morality and piety and intellectual deportment" planned for him while he was but six months old by Stockmar, the Consort's oracle; the ban upon reading fiction, lest even good Sir Walter Scott should demoralize; the isolation from boys of his own age, save for occasional meetings at Windsor Castle with selected youths from Eton made formal by the Prince Consort's unremitting presence. The Mahogany Bar is a mission hall now, and over the platform where fought the naked women a placard asks, "When did you last write home to Mother?"

It is doubtful whether Thomas Day (1748–1789), author of the *History of Sandford and Merton*, who was born in Wellclose Square, would be much company for a pleasure-loving Prince of Wales. He was, however, decidedly original.

South of Ratcliff Highway lies the riverside district of Wapping. From here Judge Jeffreys, first Baron Jeffreys of Wem and Lord Chancellor of England, tried to escape disguised as a sailor after the downfall and flight of his master. James II, who owed so much to him, actually gained credit for leaving him behind to his fate. His fate was to be recognized despite the disguise while drinking ale in the Red Cow, Anchor & Hope Alley, near King Edward's Stairs, and the manner of it furnishes a cautionary story of poetic justice.

There is a certain amount to be said for Jeffreys (1648–1689), beyond that he was a rollicking boon-companion of an evening for wine, women and song. Obviously he had great natural ability. In civil cases he displayed immense acumen, with vitality, humour and stimulating turns of speech; and it is instructive to consider how little of what he had established was overturned after his death as a suddenly disgraced and long-hated man. Where neither life nor bribery nor particular personal bias entered, he was an admirable and enjoyable judge. He had rational views on witchcraft; some honesty of conscience kept him from turning Roman Catholic; and when a youthful scheme to marry a City heiress through the help of her companion was discovered, he married the companion, who had been dismissed from her job. As to criminal trials, in Tudor and Stuart times these generally seem to us to have proceeded most cruelly upon very slim evidence. The prisoner was in a double sense on trial for his life: the underlying evidence against him was often his entire life and personality; and a jury was not necessarily bullied to its decision that, since the Government judged the fellow should be killed, why, they ought to support their Government. There was a strong presumption of guilt against anyone so indiscreet as to be arrested. For the notorious Bloody Assize in the West after Monmouth's rising, Jeffreys hanged 331, transported

849 to the American plantations, and had another thirty-three fined or flogged. The figures are not enormous for a great rebellion, but the calamity fell suddenly upon a small area, as with the bombing of Coventry, and so had an everlasting effect. To the last Lord Jeffreys did not repent of it; he asserted, and we have ample occasion to believe him, that the punishment fell short of King James's intention. He was throughout in great pain from the stone, and could not altogether have controlled if he would his rage and his invective.

Lord Jeffreys was judged a bad man in his own time and place. For all his midnight *bonhomie*—which never spared any friend at midday—he was a ferocious man. The execution of Algernon Sidney is now considered a judicial murder. Certainly there was no pressure to justify his barbarity in the case of Alice Lisle, aged eighty, in the Bloody Assize. She was accused merely of giving compassionate shelter to two fugitives from the battle of Sedgemoor. When a juryman pertinently asked whether she could be convicted for harbouring traitors before they had been judged to be such, Jeffreys, wrong technically as well as morally, said it could be so. And he sentenced her to be burnt alive. The utmost efforts of the Dean and Chapter of Winchester were needed to reduce the sentence to mere beheading. Above all, he was a born bully, a man who loved publicly to humiliate his fellows. Charles II, whom he could amuse, but who judged him unfavourably, remarked that he had "more impudence than ten carted street-walkers," and a contemporary records "His weakness was that he could not reprehend without scolding; and in such Billingsgate language as should not come out of the mouth of any man. He called it 'giving a lick with the rough side of his tongue.' . . . And they used to say, 'This is yours; my turn will be tomorrow.' He loved to insult." Now, once he so rated a scrivener of Wapping, in mere sport, that the man said afterwards, "I am escaped from the terrors of that man's face, which I would scarce undergo again to save my life; and I shall certainly have the frightful impression of it as long as I live." He recognized that face at the Red Cow in Wapping.

Jeffreys was taken to the Tower to save him from the mob; he helped the Mayor (who from respect and old acquaintance swooned and died immediately after the shock of arrest) to draw up the warrant for his own commitment. He died, aged forty-one, in little over four months, the debauched corpulence which had swallowed his handsome looks worn to skeleton thinness. The "present" of an oyster barrel containing a halter, the curses of the mob, the prisoner's passionate

Judge Jeffreys

reliance on the comfort of brandy, are well known. Among the latest of his many jokes was one made before his fall but on the edge of the precipice. When asked what were the heads in the Prince of Orange's Declaration, Jeffreys answered that "he was sure his own was one."

Edmund Spenser (*c.* 1552–1599) was born in East Smithfield; the site is number 6. His friendship with Sir Philip Sidney led, through Sidney's uncle, the Earl of Leicester, to a job in Ireland in 1580. He went as private secretary to the new Lord Deputy, Lord Grey de Wilton, who crushed an insurrection with such severity that it was felt in England to be exaggerated; in 1582 he was recalled. But Ireland was thenceforth Edmund Spenser's home and his doom. In spite of the immense fame his poetry won for him in England, he could not get a post at court or a suitable appointment anywhere in London. Once he travelled there with Sir Walter Raleigh, who had been staying with him, published the first three books of the *Faerie Queene*, celebrated a grand passion of love (his second) with the *Amoretti* and the *Epithalamion*. The *Prothalamion*, probably his last completed poem, was written on a later visit under the roof of Lord Essex. There was still nothing for it but to return to his post in Ireland, where he was most unwelcome. Spenser favoured coercion for the distressful country. He did much to increase and to create popular resentment at his occupancy of Kilcolman Castle, near Doneraile, Co. Cork. The Irish burnt him out, late in 1598. He and his household fled for their lives, arriving in London, houseless and destitute, around the turn of the year. He died exhausted on the 13th of January.

Bartholomew Close, Smithfield was the birthplace of Hogarth. We shall meet him again at his house in Leicester Square.

Thomas Otway, who had lived somewhat wretchedly, died young at a tavern called the Bull on Tower Hill. It was 14th April 1685; he was thirty-three, and one of the causes of his death was malnutrition. Though his plays were a success, yet the playhouse profits were but small, and he was a generous and a reckless spender. The men of fashion who liked his agreeable company were more ready to help him to folly than to fortune. He was at some time assisted by Nell Gwyn and by the Duchess of Portsmouth, those two whose future nourishment engaged the last consideration of Charles II. Alas, in the end even they let poor Otway starve.

The better substantiated of two contemporary stories of his death says that he saw a great friend named Blakiston murdered in the streets, that hot with grief and anger he followed the slayer on foot all the way to Dover to be revenged, that he fell ill there of a fever from the stress of his pursuit atop of long privation, and that returning to London and being heated he drank water and died after it.

Otway was, like his own heroes, weak but most passionately constant of affection, whether in friendship or in love. Such a hunt, with himself his sole prey, is quite in character. For the cup of cold water, fever or penury could drive him to it, though with debts and cares and tormented love he had taken too freely to stronger drink by the time he wrote *Venice Preserved*. Yet it is perhaps his masterpiece. Dedicated to his benefactress, Portsmouth, it provided a great part for Mrs Barry, his beloved.

The alternative tale is that he left his lodgings, famished, and entering a coffee house entreated a stranger for a shilling, saying, "I am the poet Otway." This gentleman, moved and shocked, gave him a guinea, from which he bought a roll of bread. Attacking it with a fury of hunger, he found that from long fasting he could not swallow and choked upon the first mouthful.

Elizabeth Barry (1658–1713) was a fine actress. She showed herself altogether generous and helpful when a younger woman, in whom she must have seen a rival, Mrs Bracegirdle, became her colleague. She was the Earl of Rochester's mistress. He had an odious character, but was both witty and wealthy; he was truly attached to her; she owed to his patronage and his teaching her successful stage début. She may well have preferred the amusing libertine to the handsome, penniless poet who wrote such good parts for her and once signed himself "the unfortunate and (even at this time) weeping Otway." Again, he wrote (six of his letters to her survive), "I love you more than health, or any happiness here or hereafter. Everything you do is a new charm to me; and, though I have languished for seven, long tedious years of desire, jealously and despairing, yet every minute I see you I still discover something new and more bewitching. Consider how I love you; what would not I renounce or enterprise for you. . . . Give me a word or two of comfort, or resolve never to look with common goodness on me more, for I cannot bear a kind look, and after it a cruel denial. This minute my heart aches for you; and, if I cannot have a right in yours, I wish it would ache till I could complain to you no longer. Remember poor Otway." She has recorded that when playing Monimia in his *The Orphan* she could never say the words "Poor Castalio!" without tears.

And so we come to "Julius Caesar's ill-erected tower," which does not really date from earlier than William the Conqueror. This is a place so fearful that it will be well not to linger as long as its historical interest invites, and well to gain courage by thinking first of a few pleasant things concerning it.

Here Lamb, in his school-days at Christ's Hospital, would come with other Blue Coat Boys "to pay a fifty-times repeated visit (where our individual faces should be as well known to the warden as those of his own charges) to the Lions in the Tower—to whose levée, by courtesy immemorial, we had prescriptive title to admission."

In 1604 Shakespeare and eight other actors, including the famous Richard Burbage, having received a licence from the King the previous year to act all manner of plays, "as well for the recreation of our loving subjects as for our solace and pleasure," walked from the Tower of London to Westminster in a procession which accompanied the King's formal entry into London. Each of the nine had received four and a half yards of scarlet cloth to wear as a cloak on this occasion.

On Thursday, 29th May 1533, Anne Boleyn, the first woman to be made a peeress in her own right (Marchioness of Pembroke), went by water to the Tower in a grand procession of barges with guns, pennons and banners, and two gaily decorated gunboats. On one a chorus of beautiful girls sang and played around Anne's device of a white falcon, crowned, on a mount, standing on a crown of gold encircled with red roses. On the other a great red dragon capered and twirled; surrounded by monsters and savage men, capering and twirling too and spitting out wildfire and coloured flames. Henry VIII, who had married her secretly the previous January, met her with a kiss. They slept that night at the Tower, and next day she progressed with pageantry to her coronation at Westminster. Fleet Street and Cheapside ran with wine.

But this is not why Anne, it is said, haunts the Tower—a singularly well-attested ghost, whom sentries have fainted to see.

Henry VIII was the second king to solicit Anne Boleyn; during her three years stay at the Court of France she had resisted Francois I, even when he wrote her poetry:

> Venus was blonde, have I heard tell,
> But well I see she is brunette . . .

She came back to England in 1521. Next year she and Henry Percy, the Earl of Northumberland's son, lovingly plighted their troth, asking

Anne Boleyn

Edmund Spenser

Thomas Otway

Captain Cook

Sir Richard Whittington

Daniel Defoe

Jonathan Wild

Alexander Pope

no one's leave, and Henry VIII gave Cardinal Wolsey his orders: "By God, my lord Cardinal, I would not this marriage should come to pass for twice five hundred pounds."

The Cardinal intimidated Percy, and Lord Northumberland married him off within the year. Yet he loved Anne to the end. Sent to arrest Wolsey eight years later, he was the one who showed agitation, and he could not behave well, but had his enemy's feet bound to the stirrups as though he were a common malefactor. Another six years and he found himself one of the commission of twenty-six peers ordered to find Anne guilty, with her uncle presiding; her father was most willing to have served upon it. Percy (now Northumberland) broke down and had to be helped from the court before the trial was well begun. He never recovered and did not long survive her.

Anne was made of sterner stuff. She took her broken heart from court, and nothing the King wrote or said could tempt her back to it for four years. It was a long time to leave her natural element which her graces so adorned. Several more years passed after her return before she would become the King's mistress; proceedings had then been instituted with a view to the royal divorce, and her lover could scarce endure the waiting to marry her and beget heirs. How much more brilliant her destiny seemed than that of her wilder yet gentler sister Mary. Mary was a lovely girl who married twice for mutual love without money or favour. The King took a fancy to her while Anne was still in France, and she got the thing done with safety and soon—let him come, let him go, let her detestable father take the profits. Anne was impossible to get, then hard to get, and the King's resolute love to her was marvellous. He loved her longer than the siege of Troy, and was unfaithful within three months of her coronation. When, through her transport of emotion at finding Miss Seymour on the King's knees, her boy was born prematurely and dead, it remained only to decide how to get rid of her. To the charge of adultery with four men was added a charge of incest with her brother George Boleyn, Lord Rochfort, put forward by his wife, called the infamous Lady Rochfort. And so Anne came again to the Tower, and to the room where she had slept before; but this time she came by Traitor's Gate.

Nothing was proved against any of these unfortunate people. Anne acquitted herself well at her trial, but could not be acquitted by the peers. Her distress of mind was very great that five people more or less dear to her had to perish wretchedly; Mark Smeaton the musician had been tortured. Small wonder that her ghost walks, though for herself she had ceased to care. "I hear the executioner is very good, and I have a little neck," she said.

George Boleyn on his last night at the Tower, or anywhere else on earth, wrote (for it was a period of gentle verses):

> Farewell my lute, this is the last
> Labour that thou or I shall waste,
> For ended is that we began;
> Now is the song both sung and past,
> My lute be still; for I have done.

Anne too wrote her funeral verses:

> Oh death, rock me asleep,
> Bring on my quiet rest,
> Let pass my very guiltless ghost
> Out of my careful breast. . . .

On the morning of the execution King Henry with his hounds and huntsmen waited till a gun, fired from the Tower, signalled the deed was done. The chase was so organized as to finish near where Jane Seymour lodged. He arrived that evening, and in the morning they married.

Of course many people were in and out of the Tower with no hopeless harm done. Sir Thomas Wyatt (*c.* 1503–1542), a childhood's playmate and afterwards friend and admirer of Anne Boleyn's, went to prison three times. The first visit was for a brawl between his men and some London citizens. The second occasion was upon his striking the Earl of Suffolk in May 1536, the month in which his old friend Anne was beheaded and an imprudent season for any questionable conduct from him. In May 1541, at the downfall of his patron Thomas Cromwell, he was sent to the Tower again, but even though the charge was high treason he was soon out and clear of all aspersions. He wrote Anne poems that were the perfection of grace. He and the Earl of Surrey were the first to write sonnets in our tongue. Henry VIII really liked him very much, though in their young days Wyatt was sometimes bold and merry with him to the point of rashness. It was well known that he used the King's favour chiefly to do favours for others. He could deny no one help, and it was a saying when any man received sudden advancement, "he has been in Wyatt's closet."

His father Sir Henry paid his visit to the Tower for resisting Richard III, was liberated in 1485, and lived prosperously till his death in 1537. Tradition has it that while in the Tower he had a rare experience. His dungeon was cold and narrow, he had no bed to lie on, nor enough to eat, nor sufficiency of clothes to keep him warm. One day a cat came into the place, and he coaxed her to his bosom to warm him and "by making much of her won her love." She came several times a day thereafter, sometimes bringing a pigeon. These pigeons the gaoler, very properly, would always dress without asking any questions. Sir Henry loved cats ever after, and in his portraits there was always one by his side.

Richard III saw him one day being tortured with the barnacles, and exclaimed, "Wyatt, why art thou such a fool? Thou servest for moonshine in water." And he offered him reward to forsake the ruined fugitive Henry Richmond and become his. But Wyatt answered: "If I had first chosen you for my master, thus faithful would I have been to you if you should have needed it. But the Earl, poor and unhappy though he be, he is my master."

His grandson, poor Sir Thomas Wyatt the younger, raised Kent against Mary Tudor and marched upon London. He was executed on Tower Hill in 1554, aged perhaps a little over thirty. And while he was tortured first for information, Princess Elizabeth, who was but twenty-one years of age, had the hardihood to stand on the stairs that led to the dreadful room, listening; for it was necessary for her to know exactly what was wrung from him, exactly in what way he might compromise her, lest she should be called in question unprepared.

From the Tower in July 1603, King James II having been moved by the envious to destroy him, Sir Walter Raleigh (determined to destroy himself) wrote to his wife, that Elizabeth Throgmorton whose reciprocal love for him had been so great a vexation to Queen Elizabeth:

"That I can live never to see thee and my child more!—I cannot. I have desired God and disputed with my reason, but nature and compassion hath the victory. That I can live to think how you are both left a spoil to my enemies, and that my name shall be a dishonour to my child—I cannot. I cannot endure the memory thereof. Unfortunate woman, unfortunate child. . . .

". . . I bless my poor child; and let him know his father was no traitor. Be bold of my innocence, for God—to whom I offer life and soul—knows it. And whosoever thou choose again after me, let him be thy beloved, for he is part of me and I live in him; and the difference is but in the number and not in the kind. And the Lord forever keep thee and them, and give thee comfort in both worlds."

He defended himself with great spirit, but was condemned to death, and had reached the scaffold itself before the sentence was commuted to life imprisonment. And so he lived with his wife and son in his apartments in the upper storey of the Bloody Tower, busying himself with chemical experiments and with much eloquent writing. The first and sole volume of his *History of the World* reached 130 B.C., and was suppressed as "too saucy in censuring the acts of kings." The Tower was kind compared with the release in January 1616 for a voyage to the Orinoco, where gold must be found without molesting the Spaniards. The disastrous journey out, the exhausting fever which forced him to stay behind with the ships, the sick waiting for news of his deputy, Laurence Kemys, and the command entrusted to him, all pales before the distress of the journey home. The adventurers had burned a new Spanish town, young Walter Raleigh had fallen in the fighting, no gold at all had been discovered, and Kemys had killed himself. The ship that reached Plymouth with Sir Walter in June 1618 was named the *Destiny*. He was beheaded on the 29th of October under the original sixteen-year-old sentence.

The last time the Tower was used as a state prison was in 1820 for the Cato Street Conspirators, who had been arranging to massacre all the king's ministers, but being second in the field have not attained such wide celebrity as poor Guy Fawkes.

Many worldly and many spiritual reflections have been engraved on their prison walls by occupants of the Tower throughout the centuries. Only one of them, Thomas Wyllinger, goldsmith, has engraved a memorial of love.

Perhaps no association with the Tower is more fascinating than Colonel Blood's near-success in the stylish crime of stealing the regalia in 1671. "It was a gallant attempt, however unsuccessful; it was for a crown!" he cried when seized. Though a man of infinite dash, he also had patience, and had prepared the ground well. His cultivation of good old Talbot Edwards, who was in charge of the jewels and allowed to show them to the public in lieu of salary, has some excellent touches. The parson's dress is a little obvious, but the four pairs of white gloves seem just the right thank-you present to Mrs Edwards for her kindness to Blood's bogus wife, taken with a bogus faint, and a nephew with two or three hundred pounds a year to marry the Edwards' pretty daughter was an invaluable fiction. When "Parson" Blood, his "nephew" and two friends set about the business, the old man fought so hard that they came near to killing him despite a resolve (Blood was sometimes generous) that he should be spared. But only

Colonel Blood

the unexpected, purely coincidental arrival of the Edwards' young son defeated the plan.

Charles II pardoned the forfeit life of Thomas Blood, for the Colonel represented himself as head of many disbanded soldiers, etc., who for want of liberty of conscience were all pledged to kill the King, but would be disarmed by the gesture of sparing their leader. He talked himself back into his £500-a-year estate, which he had lost at the Restoration for having sided with Parliament. It is possible that Charles thought to use him in some way; he certainly used Charles to gain privileges for old republican friends lacking to many cavaliers ruined by loyalty. The crime that brought its perpetrator £500 a year brought the stabbed and clubbed old Edwards, who had fought so well, the promise of a grant of £100 and of £50 for his prompt son. Getting the money due was considered such a toss-up that they were glad to sell their rights at half price.

II

Mainly the City; East

On Aldgate Post Office a plaque records that Geoffrey Chaucer lived there from 1374 to 1386.

Walter Thornbury, in *Old and New London*, describes the town that Chaucer knew, in the reigns of Edward IV and Richard II. "A scattered town, spotted as thick with gardens as a common meadow is with daisies. Hovels stood cheek by jowl with stately monasteries, and the fortified mansions in the narrow City lanes were surrounded by citizens' stalls and shops. Westminster Palace, out in the suburbs among fields and marshes, was joined to the City walls by that long, straggling street of bishops' and nobles' palaces, called the Strand. The Tower and the Savoy were still royal residences. In all the West-end beyond Charing Cross, and in all the north of London beyond Clerkenwell and Holborn, cows and horses grazed, milkmaids sang and ploughmen whistled. There was danger in St John's Wood and Tyburn Fields, and robbers on Hampstead Heath. The heron could be found in Marylebone pastures, and moorhens in the brooks round Paddington."

To people this landscape with human flesh and blood whose desires and emotions can reach us over the centuries, with personalities instead of the personifications and allegories of earlier writers, we had best turn to Chaucer. Almost single-handed, *The Canterbury Tales* scotch that feeling that in England real life began with the Tudors.

The Canterbury Tales, except for a few first drafts, were not written in the lodging over the gateway at Aldgate. This book was the work of later years—years, too, of disfavour and financial trouble. When Chaucer lived in Aldgate he was a flourishing man. He had his pensions, unmortgaged. His employment in the civil service took him to the wharves of Thames Street, the street where he was born. His missions in the secret service took him, not for the first time, to France, to Flanders, to Italy. He knew Genoa, Florence, Pisa, Padua; he loved the writing of Dante, Petrarch and Boccaccio, and may have met the last two. Much of his earlier work he translated and adapted first from French and afterwards from Italian literature, and there is a suggestion that he prided himself on his French accent in that little crack at the Prioress's fair and elegant command of the language:

> After the school of Stratford atte Bowe,
> For French of Paris was to her unknowe.

To this Aldgate or middle period (he was probably born about 1340 and died in 1400) belong *the Parliament of Fowls, The Legend of Good Women, Troilus and Criseyde.* A great charity runs through the works of Chaucer, down-graded perhaps to toleration in the broad and bawdy stories. He holds that man gentle whatever his birth who behaves as a gentleman. He likes and understands women, and still thinks well of them. He forgives Criseyde because she loved and because she was sorry for the harm when she proved light-weight. Cleopatra leads the "Good Women," and Medea has place among them, because they both loved.

> Hard is his heart that loveth nought
> In May, when all this mirth is wrought,

he tells us in *the Romaunt of the Rose*, and in *the Complaint of Venus* confesses:

> Now certes, Love, it is right covenable
> That men full deare buy thy noble thing.

Some of the slang words that he uses one associates more with the Victorian era—milksop, for example. That a pigges-nye or pig's eye should mean a darling reminds one of the comparatively recent cat's whiskers, cat's pyjamas, etc.

In Leadenhall Street is the church of St Katherine Cree, at which Sir John Gayer was at pains to make himself immortal. A director of the East India Company and a Lord Mayor in the reign of Charles I, he once met a lion on his trading travels and took no harm of the encounter. So much more impressed was he than was the lion, that he endowed his parish church for the provision of a "lion sermon" once a year to everlasting.

The old house of the East India Company was in Leadenhall Street. James Mill, his son John Stuart Mill and Charles Lamb all spent some time as clerks there. Each of the Mills rose to be head of his office. Lamb's policy of "making up for coming late by going away early" was not similarly rewarded.

The City is almost overwhelmingly rich in associations with memorable people.

In Cornhill, number 39 marks the site where in 1716 was born Thomas Gray, of the much loved *Elegy in a Country Churchyard.*

Sir Thomas Gresham (*c.* 1519–1579), founder of the Royal Exchange and of Gresham College, is said to have occupied a building at the corner of Cornhill and Change Alley, now replaced by Martin's Bank.

William Langland, Chaucer's contemporary, and his wife Kate had a cottage on Cornhill, and got a living by singing anniversary dirges for the dead at St Peter-upon-Cornhill. His output was small, like Gray's, being at the most two poems; *Richard the Redeless*, admonishing Richard II, is doubtfully attributed to him. His celebrated *Vision of William concerning Piers the Plowman* was a sizeable undertaking, however, not only for its length but in that he produced at least three versions. In part tedious, often arresting and beautiful, it throws some light on the life of that time:

> When I lived on Cornhill,
> Kytte and I in a cote.

Lady Mede (meaning wealth, mammon) represents Alice Perrers, the mistress of Edward III, who for avarice, covetousness and monstrous exactions was not surpassed even by Charles II's Barbara Palmer. Till Edward was on his death-bed she had the power to interest and charm and enliven him, to make tomorrow seem of hopeful meaning; and at his death-bed she stole the rings from his fingers while he was conscious and left him alone. It was natural that she was hated, but very odd that no man except the king fancied her at all.

Alexander Pope (1688–1744) was born in Plough Court, 32 Lombard Street. He once wrote in a dozen lines (*The Rape of the Lock*, Canto V) matter enough for many thousand-word women's magazine articles,

> Oh! If to dance all night and dress all day,
> Charm'd the small-pox or chas'd old age away,
> Who would not scorn what housewife's cares produce,
> Or who would learn one earthly thing of use?
> To patch, nay ogle, may become a saint;
> Nor could it sure be such a sin to paint.
> But since, alas! frail beauty must decay;
> Curl'd or uncurl'd, since locks will turn to grey;
> Since painted, or not painted, all shall fade,
> And she who scorns a man must die a maid;
> What then remains but well our power to use,
> And keep good-humour still, what e'er we lose?

Pope was aged twelve when the illness brought on by "perpetual application" ruined his health and distorted his figure. The only comforting makeweight is that he made a good deal of money and kept it. He was remarkably devious as well as vindictive and notoriously hard to get on with; but he behaved well in some situations, and had some permanent friends. John "Beggar's Opera" Gay died in his good graces. He himself was still in the Earl of Bolingbroke's good graces when the latter retired to France. Pope had had his own parlour in the Bolingbroke House, Battersea, and is said to have written there *The Essay on Man*—

"the glory, jest and riddle of the world."

And Martha Blount, to whom he left considerable property, he had known for nearly forty years.

The bitter and final quarrel with Lady Mary Wortley Montagu, whom he had formerly adored, is perhaps to some extent explained by the fact that he and she and the third party involved were all wits. (This third, John Leo Hervey, known as Lord Fanny, almost lived on ass's milk, and exclaimed, when asked to take meat at dinner, "I never eat beef or horse or any of those things.")

Where now is 43 Lombard Street was the shop of Mr Shore the goldsmith, who married a Cheapside mercer's daughter Jane. Michael Drayton (1563–1631) records Shore as "a young man of right goodly person, wealth and behaviour," who abandoned his wife after Edward IV, that handsome and cruel man, had made her his concubine. Jane Shore he describes from a painting extant in his day as short and plump and smooth and white, with a rounded face, grey eyes and dark yellow hair.

North from Lombard Street is the Moorgate Tavern, 85 Moorgate, the site of the Swan & Hoop, Finsbury Pavement, where in 1795 John Keats was born. From Finsbury Pavement to Grub (now Milton) Street once ran Ropemaker's Alley, Moorfields, where Daniel Defoe died in 1731 at the age of seventy-one; there is still a Ropemaker Street in the neighbourhood. In the same parish of St Giles, Cripplegate, he had been born, the son of a butcher named simply James Foe.

Daniel Defoe, as he styled himself, journalist, satirist and dissenter, bore arms on the side of Monmouth and later joined William III's army. He was fifty-eight when he wrote *Robinson Crusoe* and sixty when he published *Moll Flanders*, while two years later appeared his third most familiar work *The Journal of the Plague Year.*

He was about forty-three, and Queen Ann was on the throne, when he published his satirical pamphlet, *The Shortest Way with the Dissenters*, which first deceived and then infuriated the High Church party. He was sentenced to a fine, three sessions in the pillory and imprisonment in Newgate.

The pillory was a very dangerous place, owing to the whimsical humour of the mob, so justly depicted in Shakespeare's scene of the tearing of Cinna the poet. One of the few people pitied and unmolested in the pillory was the odious Titus Oates, because of the mob's ferocious hatred of Popery. One can scarcely grudge him this special immunity for, though if anyone had to endure the sentence Jeffreys laid on him one is glad it was Oates, the sentence was infamous, comparable with the knout. A less unsympathetic character, Mother Needham the procuress in Hogarth's first plate of *The Harlot's Progress*, was pelted to death by the mob in 1731; and such deaths were scarcely rare. It is a pleasure to reflect that Daniel Defoe had a triumph the very first day of his three-fold ordeal. His *Hymn to the Pillory* was a best-seller around the stocks in which he was standing, and the people drank his health.

> Hail, Hieroglyphic State Machine,
> Contrived to Punish Fancy in,

the *Hymn* begins, and continues with vigour and at length.

Further north in Finsbury is 30 Holford Square, where lived Lenin (1870–1924), founder of the U.S.S.R. At 22 Calshot Street, Finsbury, lived Joseph Grimaldi, the great pantomime clown, who was born in 1779, made his début on the stage at the age of two, and retired from it worn out with hard work in 1828, to die nine years later. Joe started at Drury Lane as the "Little Clown," mimicking his father, and became almost indispensable. Kemble did dispense with him, after a very dignified tiff. Next season the audience bawled for the famous broadsword combat, and told Kemble not to argue but to do it himself. Sheridan, present in a box, found out what had happened and reinstated Joe immediately.

South of the junction of Lombard Street and Cornhill, King William Street runs towards Billingsgate. Stow records that in 1575, at an ale-house in Smart's Quay of this district, one Wotton, formerly a gentleman and merchant of good credit, was found to be running an academy for thieves. A pocket of counters and a purse of silver were suspended with bells upon them, and on these the aspiring pickpocket had to practise his dexterity till he could empty them without a tinkle.

Westward from Lombard Street and Cornhill is the site of Thomas Hood's birthplace, the Midland Bank, Poultry. Thomas à Becket was born in Poultry or Cheapside; and Macaulay thinks that the popularity of the Canterbury pilgrimage was due not only to his character as the only canonized Englishman, but as the first man to distress the conquering dynasty.

Robert Herrick (1591–1674) was born in Cheapside. Milton was born in Bread Street between Cheapside and Cannon Street in 1608. Here, through his men or sometimes in person, Hobson, the famous carrier, would deliver Milton's home letters from the University. Hobson jobbed horses out on hire too, and was an autocratic man; his famous "choice" was that you took the nearest horse, the next due out on rotation, or no horse at all. When plague in London stopped Hobson's weekly visits he died of inactivity and boredom. Milton wrote two epigrammatic epitaphs for the occasion. Death, having for ten years "dodged with him twixt Cambridge and The Bull," at last finding him idle supposed that "now his journey's end had come."

> Rest, that gives all men life, gave him his death,
> And too much breathing put him out of breath.

Thus, in a sense, he is a London ghost. Middleton mentions him in *A Chaste Maid in Cheapside*.

In the Church of St Michael Royal, in College Hall off the south side of Cannon Street, is buried its founder, who had also a College Hill house. His immortal fame is yearly brought before the nation's notice later and longer than the infamy of poor Guy Fawkes. This citizen is Dick Whittington, who, as everyone quite rightly knows, married Alice Fitzwarren and was thrice (in fact, thrice and once over) Lord Mayor of London.

No support can be found for the pantomime's view of his early poverty and apparent insignificance, but that he amassed an immense fortune is a fact. He made kingly loans or gifts to three kings, Richard II, Henry IV and Henry V; on the last occasion a polite interchange is recorded, "Never before had subject such a king"—"Nor king such a subject!" He was also a splendid benefactor to the City, and certainly employed his wealth, wherever it came from, in a noble manner. "*Flos Mercatorum*"—"Flower of Merchants"—is all the light that his memorial tablet in St Michael's sheds on the money; and as the

William Blake

Oliver Goldsmith

Samuel Johnson

Samuel Pepys

Mr and Mrs Garrick: the Hogarth Portrait

cat still remains unaccounted for, it is tempting to try and connect them.

Legends of the master of a genuine pussy-cat coming to fortune through his dumb friend's aid can be rather widely traced in Europe. Mr Southey in his *History of the Brazils* relates that "the first pair of cats which were carried to Cuyuba sold for a pound (pound's weight) of gold. There was a plague of rats in the settlement, and they (the cats) were purchased as a speculation, which proved *an excellent one*," the first few generations of kittens holding a good though declining price. Sir William Gore Ouseley quotes a Persian MS. telling of a poor widow's son who went from Siraf to India with a cat for sole wealth, arrived at a rodent-infested palace, triumphed through his pet at the royal banquet and was magnificently rewarded. Ultimately he settled with all his family in an island named, after him, Keisor Keish. To be sure, something of the sort would not be absolutely impossible, and if it could happen once could happen again.

The funny and scurrilous Samuel Foote, whom we shall meet again in the Haymarket, produces a more liked theory in his comedy *The Nabob*. Sir Matthew Mite assures the Society of Antiquaries: "The commerce which this worthy merchant carried was chiefly confined to our coasts; for this purpose he constructed a vessel, which from its agility and lightness he aptly christened a *cat*. Nay, to this day, gentlemen, all our coals from Newcastle are imported in nothing but cats." And indeed cat was the old name for a coal or timber vessel.

There is this to be said for Foote's fancy. Sir Richard Whittington died in 1423; while he was yet a boy, the burning of coal was prohibited by Act of Parliament as a public nuisance punishable by death; a record in the Tower (Sir Everard Horne's *Dissertations*) mentions an execution for that cause; yet by 1419, when Dick had been thrice Lord Mayor of London, and without trace of the repeal of the statute, the importation of coal was an important branch of the commerce of the Thames. It would have been quite consistent with the court practises of the period if Whittington had been granted a licence to grow great by infringing the law.

In Milk Street, off Cheapside to the north, was born Thomas More, whom we associate with Chelsea; in Wood Street were born the pre-Raphaelite painter Holman Hunt, and the eminent divine and poet John Donne (1573–1631), who during his last days on earth posed in a shroud on a funeral urn for a portrait from which his monument was made.

In this district is the site of the only London house in which we know that William Shakespeare actually lodged. Any literate person can talk about Shakespeare and Shakespeare's works almost for ever—a far better conversational topic than "the musical glasses." And yet he is private to everybody; each has a secret relationship with him, and a certainty of understanding him better than can anyone else in the world. He is also private to himself; the scarcity of facts about his life is a familiar vexation, though, for what they are, they are rather satisfactory. No attempt to account for such genius can explain it; but at least he came from the class which we should expect, that middle class which has provided the overwhelming majority of our greatest poets. And at least, which we should also expect, he was thoroughly a professional man, grounded in improving and adapting plays and also in acting. We cannot forbear to expect that his colleagues liked him, and this also seems to be so. Among the few established facts of his London life, two tie up with domicile, and they are not unsympathetic: one is that he had a little tax-paying bother, and the other that he took some trouble for a family of friends in helping to arrange a marriage.

When he first came to London he found a home in the parish of St Helen's, within easy reach of "the Theatre," as James Burbage's theatre in Shoreditch was simply named; the site is 86–88 Curtain Road, Shoreditch, near Bishopsgate; and the other Shoreditch theatre called "the Curtain" was nearby. Shakespeare was put on the roll of tax-payers and became liable to an aggregate sum of £2 13*s* 4*d* for each of three subsidies voted to the Crown by Parliament in 1593. The collectors were sluggish and let it ride till he had moved south of the river to Southwark, "the Borough," in the autumn of 1596, when they caught up with him. He paid an instalment of 5*s* next year and of 13*s* 4*d* the year after; we know of no other taxes ever paid by him in London or the country; tax gathering was partial and erratic. Nor do we know how long he lived in the Borough.

From 1599 onwards he is thoroughly identified with the Globe Theatre, Bankside, Southwark. A number of his friends and colleagues lived near it, and Alleyn's theatre, "the Rose," was also on that side. But the Globe's great actor, Richard Burbage, probably went on living in Shoreditch, where he was born; he died there: his epitaph is said to have been "Exit Burbage." And Shakespeare's friends the actors John Heminge and Henry Condell lived in the heart of the City, Aldermanbury. Not far off lived the Huguenot wigmaker Christopher Mountjoy, at whose house on the corner of Silver Street and

William Shakespeare

Monkwell Street, just near Wood Street, Shakespeare is known to have stayed, how long or how briefly we cannot tell, but certainly in 1604. He was then already on intimate terms with them, and, when asked by Madam Mountjoy, acted a kindly part as go-between in arranging a match between the daughter, Mary, and the apprentice Stephen Bellott, back from a journey in Spain. After the mother's death, in 1612, when Shakespeare was mainly resident at Stratford-upon-Avon, Stephen sued Christopher for unpaid dowry, and Shakespeare as a witness in the Court of Requests signed a deposition now on view in the Public Records Office, Chancery Lane, E.C.4, where are all the documents of the case.

The Cooper's Arms, which stood on the site of the Mountjoy house, was destroyed by bombs with all Monkwell Street and almost the whole of Silver Street. But the world endures; the ground remains upon which was a house where Shakespeare is known to have lodged; where, even, he may have lodged for years, may have written some of his greatest plays; or where he may have been but a brief, occasional visitor from Bankside.

Nearby, at the bombed church of St Mary the Virgin, Aldermanbury, is that most moving monument to Heminge and Condell, to whose "disinterested affection the world owes all that it calls Shakespeare. They alone collected his dramatic writings regardless of pecuniary loss, and without the hope of any profit gave them to the World. They thus merited the gratitude of mankind." This they did—which the author, so far as we know, never took heed for—giving away their private rights in his manuscripts "onely to keepe the memory of so worthy a Friend and Fellow alive, as was our Shakespeare." And so their names are immortal, not through Condell's nine children nor even Heminge's fourteen.

To St Paul's Cathedral, Wren from the age of thirty-six till his death at ninety devoted heart and soul. During his last five years, deposed from authority and under a cloud, but "as well pleased to die in the shade as to live in the light," he had himself annually carried from his Hampton Court retirement to sit under his dome; very quiet and of high courage.

One of those condemned to do penance in the churchyard of pre-Wren St Paul's was "Edward's Miss" as Pope calls Jane Shore in his epilogue to Rowe's play—for that is how "Miss" was used in his time, and all actresses were Mrs or Mistress on the playbills. Michael Drayton says Richard III commanded that no man should relieve her, and an old ballad describes her as starving to death and perishing in a ditch, from which the name Shoreditch was derived,

> which is a witness of my sinne
> For being concubine to a king.

But Shoreditch was named much earlier, and Sir Thomas More tells us that Jane was still alive in the reign of Henry VII. He describes how her penance was pitied by the onlookers because she was so beautiful and so embarrassed, and because no one ascribed any good intent or hatred of sin to her persecutor. He records too that she used her influence for kindly ends, and he thus describes her personality:

> "Now is she old, lean, withered and dried up. . . . And yet, being even such, whoso well advise her visage, might guess and devine which parts, how filled would make it a fair face. Yet delighted men not so much in her beauty as in her pleasant behaviour. For a proper wit had she, and could both read well and write, merry in company, ready and quick of answer, neither mute nor full of babble, sometimes taunting without displeasure, and not without disport."

The old Newgate Prison no longer exists, but it is hard to walk down Newgate Street and not remember it; it was finally demolished in 1902 and some of its stones were used in the Central Criminal Court, which replaced it. Public executions took place in front of it from 1783 (when it superseded Tyburn) to 1868.

Here Elizabeth Fry began those endeavours which were the foundation of prison reform throughout Europe.

Here Jane Webb was committed. She was known as Jenny Diver, and was worth a good deal more than Gay's Jenny Diver in *The Beggar's Opera*. Her good taste in appearance and demureness in manner were similar, but she was no traitor. At the start of her criminal career, at the age of fourteen, she sent his clothes and money after an accomplice who got caught. She closed that career at the age of thirty-five, going so resolutely to the rescue of a male accomplice who had been seized upon that he did indeed escape, leaving her and another female thief to destruction. One of Jenny's last cares was to protest the innocence of this companion so strongly that the sentence was mitigated to transportation. She herself went to Tyburn, on 18th March 1740, with that distinction which ever marked her. Her fame was such that a rescue was feared; so, after the seven carts of malefactors (each with his or her coffin, and a rope worn around the neck), Jenny rode in a mourning coach, guarded by musketeers, Light Horse and forty infantry.

All feminists should reverence Jenny, since at the age of seventeen she was chosen leader by a gang of experienced and tough criminals, predominantly male. And she really led. Her dexterity was amazing. So was her ingenuity; she would successfully use such devices as a false pair of arms to be conspicuously folded in church over a pregnancy of cushions, while her own hands wandered; or devise a whole drama of deceit to be acted by her band, for the luring and depriving of a lecherous gallant in a playhouse. She drew up a sound and democratic thieves' charter. Against her is that she would play upon the most truly charitable feelings of her victims; for her is that, aside from such individual charitable feelings, society would see her starve unaided, its provisions being all in savage defence of property. As a Newgate chaplain said, such people as Jenny dated their lives not by years but by sessions.

A pamphlet published in 1621 is entitled "The wonderfull discoverie of Elizabeth Sawyer, a witch late of Edmonton; her conviction, her condemnation and death; together with the relation of the Devil's accesse to her, and their conference together. Written by Henry Goodcote, minister of the Word of God, and her continual visitor in the Gaole of Newgate."

The play founded upon this unfortunate by Dekker, Ford and Rowley, probably first performed in 1623 but not published till 1658, gives a powerful picture of a poor, warped old woman called a witch before she is one and hounded to the devil by her neighbours. Like Shylock, like Vittoria Corombona, she is given telling things to say in self-defence before she is confounded. In this play we have also one of the earliest appearances of a figure we scarcely meet again till du Maurier's Trilby—the tarnished heroine who is redeemed by a pure, gentle love (no Cleopatra, she) without the fuss of an orgy of grief and penitence (unlike Little Em'ly) and with the author's full approval. Another gentle feature of *The Witch of Edmonton* is the compunction of Cuddy Banks for the witch's familiar because he takes the form of a dog, and his anxiety to find him honest yet profitable employment in any canine shape he might be coaxed to assume and retain.

Dekker, of Dutch origin perhaps, but a Londoner born and bred, haunts the City, an exceedingly good-humoured shade, full of fancy, gaiety and tender affection, retaining by the grace of God his poetry, his touch of genius, while "as men would serve a cowcumber" he throws himself away.

He collaborated with almost everyone save Shakespeare; Ben Jonson, with whom he afterwards jangled not too spitefully, Drayton, Middleton, Ford—as we have seen—and Massinger (seven of whose plays, in the possession of Mr Warburton, were burnt leaf after leaf as covers for pie-crust by Mr Warburton's cook). Dekker was something of a journalist like many of his brilliant contemporaries; pressed by urgency of special occasions and of debts into hack work not intended for resurrection. He was more than once in prison for debt. A prolific writer, he took little heed to publishing his plays; he was befriended by the wealthy Alleyn; he underrated his own talent. We know not the date of his birth nor the date and manner of his death. But we know his London. In his pleasantly satirical *The Gull's Horn Book* we follow a young gallant about the ordinary, the playhouse, the tavern, the rowdily profaned middle aisle of St Pauls. *The Shoemaker's Holiday* is laid around Tower Street, Old Ford and Cornhill, the Boar's Head and the Swan; among the young journeymen, sturdily ready to go on strike for injustice to a fellow, yet quickly reconciled; and presents as poetic and delicate a love between one young journeyman and his seamstress wife as ever he could have given to a lord and lady. The poem *Dekker his Dream*, which sometimes breaks into prose, throws light on his life and reveals his imagination.

> Each man was both the lion and the prey,
> And every cornfield an Aseldema.

"There is a Hell named in our Creed, and a Heaven, and the Hell comes before; if we look not into the first, we shall never live in the last." It does not need his account of plague or of the misery of prison to guess that somewhere, somehow this merry and tender poet had his glance or two into the hell that can be on earth.

Among other lodgers at Newgate were poor Anne Askew; Jack Sheppard, the thieving young carpenter, who after his second and most daringly expert escape from the prison was easily recaptured getting dead drunk with his mother; and Jonathan Wild, hanged in 1725, who lived so conveniently just round the corner, first at 68 and then at a grander house on the other side in Old Bailey—the street where Milton's defence of Charles I's execution was burnt by the common hangman.

Jonathan Wild was so great an organizing genius, so brilliant a ruler of men and women that one could wish Fielding had written his real history instead of borrowing his name—a capital name—for fiction. He was a wicked man, really wicked, not just a criminal, like charming Jenny Diver; and that the king of fences should boast and advertise himself as The Thief-taker does not immediately endear. That he did inform on and help to send to the gallows several dozen robbers, pick-pockets, returned convicts, etc., is unquestionable, nor does it seem that he stopped short of framing some of them by plot and perjury. However, it is easy to misunderstand this activity, which was not primarily a matter either of spite or of the official monetary reward.

That he advertised it gives us a clue—paying newspapers, standing treat to condemned men who would promise to mention his blood-hound rôle in their speeches at the gallows. It was necessary to him and to all his operatives that he should have status with the authorities responsible for maintaining the law. It was also necessary to make an occasional example, for the sake of reliable dealing and his own authority. A dissipated cheesemonger, ruined, without resources or patron, was rescued by Wild as Fagin rescued waifs who could have died in the streets but for his roof, his blazing fire, his sausages. Wild gave a talk on highway robbery without tears, bought the poor fellow a horse, and set him in a fair way to a new business. The cheesemonger succeeded well on the roads, but failed to give Wild the promised percentage. Wild rode out, found him, and without a word of reproach for his ungrateful parsimony shot him dead; then reported he had done the State some service. But enemies and double-crossers were especially useful when some loyal thief of Wild's own gang was arrested. The best way to get such a friend off was to furnish him or her with material for turning king's evidence, so that many marked men were spared for a while to this purpose, briefly living in a fool's paradise.

Jonothan Wild was born in Wolverhampton in 1682, son to a peruke-maker, later apprentice to a buckle-maker. He served his time, married, had a son, went on a business visit to London, got employment in his trade, found town life expensive, and was arrested for debt. This young fellow from the country was thrown into the Wood Street Comptor for four years. He may have come out with a grudge against society; he certainly came out with Mary Milliner, prostitute and pick-pocket, who helped him to the first rung of that ladder on which he climbed to heights where she could not follow. In due course he set her up as mistress of a small house in Moorfields, and could be counted on ever after to help her when she needed cash. He married bigamously a succession of wives, and treated them handsomely; the last had a liveried footman to attend her walks abroad, and they dined each day on five courses—not forgetting to send the remains to the prisoners on the common-felon side of Newgate gaol.

It was wholly a compliment to Wild that in 1717, for the first time, receivers of stolen goods were put in danger of the law. On that, he merely changed his business to that of a restorer of stolen goods. He would happen to have heard of someone's loss and happen by hazard to have wind of the property's whereabouts, and a notion would occur to him by which through a present to somebody the goods could be recovered. Soon he opened an agency at which the victims would register with him on payment of a booking fee. Meanwhile common thieves were being taught to extend their activities to objects previously worthless, such as ships' documents, merchants' account books and ladies' keepsakes; while the "spruce prigs" chosen to mingle with the world of fashion were hard at it learning dancing and deportment.

Honesty in his calling was no doubt the best policy. He always gave the goods for the money and always divided the money handsomely. Though he did not even spare his old friend Joseph Blake, or "Blueskin," on finding himself defied and included out by Blueskin and Jack Sheppard, he was not always implacable to repentance. His last chapter began by his efforts to play peacemaker between two rogues (he disliked quarrels) and by the gallant rescue of one of them, Roger Johnson, from the law. This Johnson's disposition to quarrel had earlier cost Wild a promising business sideline and a fine of £700, but he had not been disloyal, so he was rescued and Wild was arrested and a case on other charges prepared against him.

Jonathan Wild had promised Blueskin, waiting for execution less than a year earlier, "I'll send you a good book or two, and provide you with a coffin, and you shall not be anatomised." Though Blueskin did mind about his mortal frame, he was not grateful, and on one visit from his old colleague went for his throat with a knife—a blunt one, as it happened. Wild does not seem to have worried about his own funeral. He asked what was meant by the text "Cursed is everyone that hangeth on a tree" and what was the state of the soul departed from the body, but was told to think of serious things. On his last evening he discussed suicide, and must have read a few good books in his day, for he cited various noble Greeks and Romans. Owning himself beaten in argument, he yet took laudanum, but was saved by the officious kindness of fellow prisoners for the ride to Tyburn, much cursed and pelted with mud and stones by the mob who did not appreciate him. He had reckoned his life more securely than session by session. He had not believed that it would come to this, and he made a baffled, brooding sort of exit.

Old Bailey runs down to the west end of Ludgate Hill. Off Ludgate Hill is La Belle Sauvage Yard where stood the famous Bell Sauvage Inn, called also Savage's Inn. The George in Southwark is the only inn of that period left in London, and the Belle Sauvage must have looked something like it. In the yard, with its galleries, plays were performed; there was, too, a school of fencing in Queen Elizabeth's day; and here it was that Banks, the showman, mentioned in Elizabethan pamphlets by Nash and others, charmed the audiences with Marocco, his wonderful trained horse. Marocco once ascended St Paul's spire. Once he delighted all by picking on Tarleton, the celebrated clown (who may have been Shakespeare's Yorick), when his master asked him who was the greatest fool there. One day Banks the showman with Marocco the horse, proudly shod in silver, went to Rome in bright hope to make their fortunes. They were too good. The tricks frightened the priests, who took the precaution of burning them both for witchcraft. They died for no cause of their own defending, for no spite's satisfaction and no man's gain. The violence was implacable but well-intentioned. One can almost hear the walls of the world dripping blood and see it sprinkled in the meadows.

Grinling Gibbons lived in La Belle Sauvage Yard, his sign a carved pot of wooden flowers so light and airy that they shook to the sound of coaches. Hard by lived the scornful cobbler (mentioned by Steele) who bought the wooden figure of a beau of the time, bent humbly before him, patiently offering the tools of the shoemaker's craft.

III

Mainly the City; West

Dante Gabriel Rossetti's "crib" in Blackfairs, 14 Chatham Place, was a pre-Embankment lodging, right upon the river and with a balcony. At high tide in the sun of summer it must have been brilliantly enchanting, at low tide the mud banks smelt of decay, in damp weather miasma sealed it for its own. He kept the place from 1853 till Lizzie Siddal's death in 1862—Lizzie Rossetti of two years' standing, as she was then, after ten years' previous association.

Rossetti had romantic or sensual relations with a redhead, a blonde and a brunette; in his fashion he was faithful till the grave to all three. The blonde professional model, Fanny Cornforth (originally—just as good a name—Sarah Cox), was on a different plane from Lizzie; we could be bold and say a lower plane; though not to be belittled, for her "Rhinoceros" really *liked* his common and justly mercenary "Elephant"; always, even when better friends became suspect and misunderstood. For Elizabeth Siddal, the Beatrice to Rossetti's Dante, it may well have been harder to forgive his attachment to Jane Burden, spiritual as well as beautiful, who married William (Topsy) Morris—perhaps at Gabriel's desperate request? For when he met Jane Burden in 1857 he felt himself hopelessly committed to Miss Siddal; he might hedge and hedge with her, but could not find courage for a new plan, a getaway, a fresh start. Yet Jane's marriage in 1859 (the year before his own wedding) to Morris, who adored her, kept her at least in the Pre-Raphaelite Circle—the half loaf that is better than no bread. Already Rossetti and Lizzie Siddal had failed in their timing. First she had delayed too long in yielding to seduction, then he had delayed too long in yielding to marriage. By then she had been a ghost woman for years, isolated by physical decline and suffering.

The attraction (not so usual as supposed) was of opposites. The young Rossetti was warm and virile, wayward and merry, with the gift to fascinate and to dominate and to make fun of all things. (He had a fine vein of sheer gaiety and of pure nonsense; though that simple, hearty pre-Raphaelite fun, he and Ruskin hiding each other's paints and roaring with laughter, etc., strikes a tiresome note even as a prelude to

Dante Gabriel Rossetti

so much doom.) Miss Siddal was cold and apathetic, remote and ethereal, yet she warmed to a flowering of pent-up talent at his Svengali-touch, and was by no means incapable of the hysterical scene. Of course she was not always drifting or brooding or suffering. She used to tease Swinburne charmingly, and made a bond of jokes between them about their red hair. Everyone liked her, considered her a stunner, as they called attractive women. "Beautiful, wonderful Guggums!" exclaimed one of the circle—for this, alas, was Rossetti's name for her, neither pretty nor even private, while he to match it was Gug. They took no decision, made no bold bid in the high noon of love, and pain persuaded after joy had failed.

She was as fatal to him as he to her. For her the still-born baby; the irritation and pain that laudanum dulled; the dreadful separateness, the exile of ill-health; the jealous pangs; the fatal dose at last. For him that agony of grief and remorse which dictated the gesture of burying his little manuscript book of poems in the glory of her coffined red hair—remorse which was still his grim companion when seven years later he consented to exhumation and deciphered for the publishers pages touched here and there by mortal decay. There were good times ahead too; the brilliant Bohemian magic which he created so untidily in Chelsea; but he had need of Fanny and of Jane, for the dead Lizzie never left him. He is a figure with great power to haunt (after his visit to Penkill Castle in Ayrshire he could still be heard for the rest of the season reading aloud to himself above the drawing-room each evening in an empty room), but he is certainly a haunted ghost. We shall not know if it would have been a better thing to have married Jane Burden.

Not far away, in Shoe Lane, lived at another time John Florio. The Earls of Southampton and Pembroke were his benefactors and he was well known; it is therefore reasonable conjecture, though no more, to suppose that Shakespeare met him; it is almost sure that Shakespeare, as well as Ben Jonson, read his translation of the essays of Montaigne. This translation (despite some embroideries from a lover of words, and some inaccuracies, such as confusion between the French for book and for hare) is unsurpassed both in spirit or beauty. Florio prospered. No ironic or cruel end awaited the translator of the beautiful and loving essay against cruelty.

In Gunpowder Alley off Shoe Lane, Richard Lovelace died two years before the Restoration, an exquisite, limited poet and exemplary cavalier. Anthony Wood tells us that when presented, aged sixteen, at the court of Charles I he was "the most amiable and beautiful youth eye ever beheld. A person, also, of innate modesty, virtue and courtly deportment, which made him then, but especially after, when he retired to the great city, much admired and adored by the fair sex." Twice he was imprisoned, and in his last ten years he who had worn cloth of gold and of silver raggedly haunted obscure and shabby places such as the alley of his death, debouching from Shoe Lane.

In Gunpowder Alley in Cromwell's time (he was consulted by both sides) lived Lilly, astrologer, cheat, possibly real medium, and protégé of the angel Salmonaeus. He wrote wittily of his Welsh tutor from Staffordshire, Evans, who had settled in the same alley, and described with spirit a treasure-hunt in the cloisters of Westminster from which he was driven by a storm created by demons. He produced an almanach every year and died in his bed in 1681 at the mature age of 79—unlike poor John Lambe, the Wood Street "conjuror," who fifty-three years earlier was quite pointlessly and haphazardly lynched by a mob of apprentices, and only rescued to die. True he had just spent fifteen years in prison for "execrable arts, and, worse still, was protected by the Duke of Buckingham."

Samuel Pepys was born where now is Salisbury Court, Fleet Street, the son of a tailor, and at twenty-two married a pretty girl of fifteen whom he often vexed but who must have had a good deal of fun with him. Apart from our debt to him for his intelligent interest in the theatre, his lively curiosity, sharp observation, retentive memory and racy style, he is to be honoured as a most competent and conscientious official who set about reforming abuses energetically in an age when these virtues were not the fashion, and who stuck to his post through the long, grisly months of the plague. Certainly he is an immortal Londoner, for what he has told us about his London and for what he has revealed to us about himself—a better man, after all, than many who are graver.

Doctor Samuel Johnson (1709–1784) had many lodgings in London. The site of a house in Johnson's Court (so named already when he went there) off Fleet Street, where he lived from 1765–1776, is marked with a plaque. Staple Inn, where he wrote *Rasselas* to pay for his mother's funeral, has suffered serious war damage, and Johnson's rooms there may, indeed, have been demolished earlier. The house in Bolt Court where he died was burnt down thirty-five years afterwards. Nor does 1 Inner Temple Lane, where he had his early meetings with Boswell, exist any more; it was probably there that William Fitzherbert, M.P. for Derby, dropped in to write a letter and was surprised to find no paper, no ink and no pen. It was Fitzherbert whom Johnson used to cite as proof that "a man will please more upon the whole by negative than positive qualities."

The house where Doctor Johnson resided from 1748 till 1759 is unspoilt and on show; 17 Gough Square, where with the aid of six amanuenses he compiled his dictionary, and included "a harmless drudge" among the definitions of the word lexicographer.

Johnson, with his love of Fleet Street and of good company, his wide interests, his gift for conviviality and appreciation, his profound, irretrievable unhappiness and dreadful fear of death, is unquestioned as a famous London ghost. He wrote of the long, intimate association with the Thrales that it had "soothed twenty years of a life radically wretched." Naturally he had a good opinion of innocent pleasure and amusements, those valuable human standbys. One can hardly bear that rain should have disappointed him of a promised display of Torre's fireworks at Mr Gough's Marylebone Gardens—in vain he incited some young men to light the waterlogged wrecks; few of the wheels and stars and suns would blaze to give him comfort. The pleasure grounds of Vauxhall (much praised by Boswell) and Ranelagh were the other smartest open-air places of resort; Ranelagh was destined to eclipse its rival on the other side of the water, and in 1744 Horace Walpole wrote that Lord Chesterfield liked it so well he had ordered all his correspondence to be sent there. When someone remarked to Johnson that, for all the music and dancing and frescoes and illuminations, the marvellous rotunda, the Venetian pavilion in the lake, the sequestered alcoves, the sweet-scented shrubs and the fairy-tale effects, there was not half a guinea's worth of pleasure in seeing Ranelagh, Johnson smartly replied: "No; but there is half a guinea's worth of inferiority to other people in not having seen it." He had also said something less smart and more touching: "When I first entered Ranelagh it gave an expansion and gay sensation to my mind, such as I never experienced anywhere else."

One of the period's recreations was never patronised by Doctor Johnson; he did not go to public executions. Boswell, like George Selwyn, had a passion for them, and certainly they were great dramas. Though Johnson would not go, he took a conservative line and objected strongly when, late in 1783, it was decided to spare the condemned their journey in carts through the mob from Newgate to

Tyburn and to execute them outside the prison instead. "Tyburn itself is not safe from the fury of innovation," said the doctor.

He visited Bedlam, where twopence would let you into a maniac's cell, a couple of times. The first time he went in none too scrupulous company, with Samuel Foote the actor and outrageous mimic, and Alexander Wedderburn, the able but venal advocate. Wedderburn became first Earl of Rosslyn and Lord High Chancellor, and at Thomas Sheridan's suggestion got Johnson his yearly pension of £300 in 1762 through his influence with Prime Minister Bute.

Also in Gough Square, but somewhat earlier, lived a surgeon who, having one day bought a body for dissection from among those hanged at Tyburn, was startled by his little servant girl's cry that the corpse (for she had stolen a peep, and nearly thrown herself downstairs in terror) was sitting up on its board and looking vaguely round. The surgeon behaved with great generosity. He hid this—in a sense—disappointing purchase safely in his house till he could fit him out and ship him to America. The rescued man was clever, energetic and even grateful. He made the most of his new start, piled up a fortune in America, predeceased his benefactor and left him his wealth. There is one good moral; now comes another. The Gough Square surgeon died without known heir, his lawyer advertised for one and eventually established the claim of an Islington shoemaker to the fortune. The shoemaker thereupon refused to pay the lawyer's fees and tried to justify himself by calling him rogue. It was a false economy, a costly insult. The lawyer said: "I have put you into possession of this property by my exertions, now I will spend £100 out of my own pocket to take it away again, for you are not deserving of it." He advertised again for the surgeon's next of kin, and Mr Willcocks, a Strand bookseller. remembered that his wife and her mother had used to visit the house in Gough Square. Sure enough, Mrs Willcocks was proved the heir and the shoemaker was disinherited.

In 1737, Samuel Johnson aged twenty-eight and David Garrick, his pupil, aged twenty came from Lichfield to London to find their fortunes and were good-naturedly lent £5 on their joint note by Mr Willcocks, the Strand bookseller, whose wife had come into the Gough Square surgeon's fortune, much of it earned for him by his Tyburn bargain.

William Hazlitt lived in 1829 where now is 6 Bouverie Street, and it was at 9 Southampton Buildings, Chancery Lane (now premises of the Westminster Bank), that in 1820 he lodged with the Walkers—a tailor, his wife and two daughters—and conceived that passion for the girl Sarah Walker which found expression in the frantic *Liber Amoris*, 1823. The divorce from his first wife, Sarah Stoddart, was effected quite amicably in Edinburgh. In 1824 he married a charming widow, Mrs Bridgewater, who had £300 a year. They at once set off on a continental tour, and on the homeward journey she left him for ever.

Goldsmith's chambers at 2 Brick Court in the Temple have been destroyed by bombardment. They cost him £400, and from the partial success of *The Good-natured Man* he bought also Wilton carpets and blue merino curtains and fine silk clothes ornamented with gilt buttons. Reynolds, who had painted his portrait, called one day to find him kicking a parcelled-up masquerade dress around the room in despair at the folly of his own extravagance. Yet he would sup frugally off boiled milk that he might be able to give to others. He had no sense of proportion with money, no real grip of it—one of the great sources of misery in the world. How naturally comes a little extravagance from one who had had such hard times and done so much hack work: proof correcting for Richardson's press—that moral Richardson of whom Johnson remarked that he had little conversation except about his own works, and of whose fretful vanity Boswell made fun; later drudging for the publisher Mr Newberry, not altogether a hard task-master.

Goldsmith's charity was very great; it was more than a matter of squandering money, of finding it hard to say no; his time, his sympathy, his efforts to console and amuse were at the service of unfortunate fellow-Irishmen and of the London poor.

There was plenty of fun in 2 Brick Court. The lawyer below complained bitterly of the singing, the dancing, the blind-man's-buff and forfeits when Goldsmith entertained his friends. When he died, £2,000 in debt ("Is your mind at ease?" asked the doctor. "No, it is not," were the last words of Goldsmith), the staircase was blocked with wretched outcasts mourning for one whose kindness had never failed. The Temple Gardens rooks, whom he had loved and whose "plans of policy" it had amused him to watch, went about their business; but Reynolds laid his brush aside and left his painting room for the day and Burke burst into tears.

Mackworth Praed died in the same house in 1839, and for a short while in 1855 Thackeray lodged there, much moved by the kind associations with Goldsmith.

Only the entrance to Fountain Court remains; the houses are gone. William Blake (1757–1827) had two little rooms there at the end of his life, which, said his friend Samuel Palmer, he made more attractive than the threshhold of princes. Here he lay dying on an August evening when, a little before the end, a neighbour heard him "singing songs to melodies that were the inspiration of the moment." And so he died somewhat like the Lady of Shallott. Although he had suffered, had indeed passed through the dark night of the soul, he had upon the whole a happy life, inspired, doing what he wanted to do, able to make the means to live, and most singularly blest in a happy marriage of which almost all of us would have prophesied grief.

Samuel Rogers (1763–1855), poet, connoisseur, and acquaintance of most contemporary men of letters, once lived in the Temple. He tells a story in his *Table-Talk* disorienting to those reared on Kingsley's *Water Babies* and charmed by Benjamin Britten's *Let's Make an Opera.*

> "The chimneys of one of my neighbours were to be swept. Up went two boys; and at the end of an hour they had not come down again. Two other boys were then sent up; and up they remained also. The master of the boys was now summoned, who, on his arrival, exclaimed, 'Oh, the idle little rascals! They are playing at all-fours on the top of the chimney.' And, to be sure, there they were, trumping it away at their ease."

Charles Lamb moved to the Temple at the end of 1799 and stayed for about seventeen years, first at Mitre Court Buildings and then in Middle Temple Lane, offering cold beef and porter and a great deal of wit and fun every Wednesday evening to whatever friends chose to come. (The later "gin and jokes" parties at 20 Russell Street, Covent Garden, were by invitation and on no regular evening.)

Leigh Hunt said he could have imagined Lamb "cracking a joke in the teeth of a ghost, and then melting into thin air himself out of sympathy with the awful." Wordsworth spoke with emotion of his goodness and alluded to him as "Lamb, the frolic and the gentle," which was quite apt, but would have infuriated him. He once wrote to his old school friend Coleridge in something like a rage for "terming me gentle-hearted" in print; it suggested poor-spirited to him—and that he was not. Moreover, he would really try to antagonize and make a bad impression upon strangers whose personalities did not please him. He did this to Carlyle, who must be excluded from the crowd of those who loved him.

There is no question but that Lamb was lovable, one of the best-loved men there have ever been; and very funny and gay in spite of troubles. He drank a little too much, but only a little. Hazlitt has left lively accounts of the Temple evenings; Hazlitt was a regular visitor and so was Lamb's old school-fellow Coleridge. "Did you ever hear me preach?" Coleridge once asked Lamb, and Lamb, with his little stammer, replied: "I n-never heard you do anything else." Coleridge was a fabulous talker. He held Hazlitt spell-bound for a six-mile walk of ceaseless speech; he talked to Samuel Rogers for three hours about poetry without intermission, so admirably that Rogers wished for every word in writing. But sometimes such harangues were unintelligible as well as interminable; and Rogers also tells how Wordsworth, after listening politely with profound attention for two uninterrupted hours, nodding his head every now and then as though to agree, confided to him privately that he had not understood a syllable. Lamb would not have put up with it. Once when Coleridge seized him by a button and got into full relentless swing, Lamb liberated himself by cutting off the button and going off, returning later to find his friend still holding the button and still talking. At any rate, that is a Lamb's tale.

Thomas Erskine (1750–1823), who became Lord Chancellor and the first Baron Erskine of Restormel in 1806, resided at one time at 11 Sargeant's Inn. When he was an all-but-briefless young barrister he suddenly got a chance and spoke with such amazing eloquence and energy for a Captain Baillie that he went home with sixty-seven retaining fees in his pocket. His speaking never had much influence on the House of Commons; but with a jury he couldn't go wrong and became quite recklessly self-confident, belittling unexpected unanswerable evidence for the other side by winks and confidential grimaces and even addressing the good men and true as "my dear little twelvers." Tom Paine was one of the clients he successfully defended. On the 20th October 1794, after his great defence, Horne Tooke was acquitted of high treason, and a roaring rabble of Tooke supporters took the horses from Erskine's carriage in order to drag it themselves all the way from Westminster Hall to his home. Lord Eldon, another interesting legal figure of the day, on hearing of this immediately enquired whether they had ever given the horses back again.

Erskine was highly esteemed for wit as well as for eloquence, and was certainly merry and full of jokes and puns and stories. He told of a friend cured of the most stubborn insomnia by being dressed as a watchman and put with a lantern in a sentry box; he composed an epigram:

> The French have taste in all they do,
> Which we are quite without;
> For Nature, that to them gave goût,
> To us gave only gout.

He was in favour of negro emancipation and Greek independence, and wanted an Act of Parliament passed to forbid cruelty to animals. When he was at the bar, his favourite dogs went to all his consultations, another he had rescued from hooligans, and he would not see a horse beaten without protest. Later at the Hampstead house next the Spaniards, where he keenly dug and planted, he had, among other creatures, a pet goose that followed him affectionately, a favourite macaw, and two leeches which had been used to bleed him when dangerously ill at Portsmouth, and which he had therefore brought back with him from gratitude, changing their water every day and cherishing them. He thought that they knew him and had regard for him and that their dispositions were quite distinct; Clive and Howe were their names, after celebrated surgeons.

Lord Erskine said that when the hour came when all secrets should be revealed, we should know at least, wherever we might be, why shoes are always made too tight.

At 39 Brooke Street, Gray's Inn Road, Holborn, died the eighteen-year-old Thomas Chatterton in 1770, having taken arsenic in desperation at his poverty and distress.

The Bishops of Ely had once a great estate in Holborn, and it was on Holborn Hill in the late 1600's that two bailiffs caught Joe Hains, the brilliant comedian, for a debt of £20. They had no respect for his pretence to be a Count, but when he saw the Bishop of Ely approach in his carriage, claimed him for a cousin, and poked his head boldly through the window, they began to be a little impressed. What Hains said to the Bishop, whom he had never met, was that here were two Roman Catholics almost converted to Protestantism, but troubled with some last scruples. Much intrigued, the Bishop called to the bailiffs, "My friends, if you will come presently to my house, I will satisfy you in this matter." They came. And when the Bishop found what the matter really was, he did satisfy them by paying the actor's debts.

In 1856 Rossetti, twenty-eight but already a maestro, found rooms at 17 Red Lion Square, Holborn, for the young men Edward Burne-Jones and William Morris, aged twenty-three and twenty-two. Here

Lord Erskine

he came often to stay with them. Here the good little maid, Red Lion Mary, was ready to rig up packing-case beds for any stray guests, never resenting the general confusion as to work and pleasure and meal-times. Here spirits expanded, hearts were light, and there was happiness.

Rossetti was the dazzler, the younger men the dazzled. Even when slovenly, ill and physically revolting in his later years he was not without fascination; now he was all magnetism. He was extremely popular at the Working Men's College to which Ruskin took him; with no idea of moral or social improvement, he did think it natural that they must all want to paint. In the background was the weight of Lizzie's illness, her unsuccessful journeys here or there to get well, Ruskin's extreme delicacy and kindness in financial or any help concerning her, Ruskin's intolerable insistence on telling Rossetti how to do his own work (after Lizzie's death, Rossetti would never see that great prophet, that beautiful and lucid writer again). In the foreground was the three-fold friendship, the painting, the freedom, the visits to theatres, to the Zoo, to the Madox-Browns, to the Brownings, to Holland House, to the show called "Judge and Jury" where the audience, comfortably drinking, was the jury, while "Baron" Renton Nicholson dressed as a judge conducted (with considerable licence) a mock trial on some *cause célèbre* of the day—for preference crim. con. (criminal conversation), as adultery was called. Better than a play, said Rossetti. And literally blocking the foreground was Morris's "intensely mediaeval furniture . . . tables and chairs like incubi and succubi."

Burne-Jones and Morris stayed there till 1859: the year when Morris married Jane Burden; the year when a sort of home-guard was formed on an anti-French scare, and Leighton, Millais, Holman Hunt, Watts, Swinburne, Rossetti, Burne-Jones and Morris all found themselves in the Artists' Rifles with Ruskin as an honorary member. When told to form fours, Rossetti asked, "Why?"

The house still stands, a memorial of that particular kind of once-in-a-lifetime happiness which all who have ever known it recognize in Burne-Jones's well-known description of 1856: "There was a year in which I think it never rained, nor clouded, but was blue summer from Christmas to Christmas, and London streets glittered, and it was always morning, and the air sweet and full of bells."

IV

North; St Pancras, Highgate, Hampstead, St John's Wood, St Marylebone, etcetera

We have left the City already and crossed to Holborn, so may conveniently strike north, beginning with St Pancras.

14 Doughty Street, Mecklenburgh Square (formerly 8), is the first of Sydney Smith's London houses; he stayed from 1803 till 1806. Though grief fell upon the place shortly after his arrival and he lost a son almost at birth, and though he was harassed by poverty, there was much merriment, great pleasantness and even happiness. This bold, incisive, liberal-minded creator of the *Edinburgh Review* had tearing high spirits of the most spontaneous kind, and adored London, where he was also immensely popular. But most of his life was passed in the country, which he considered a kind of "healthy grave."

He was a clergyman of little doctrine, most complete in charity, courage and honesty. He was the equal of Yorick in his own line, and threw Mrs Siddons from her deliberate, dignified gravity into such convulsions that she had to be helped from the table. Even when he lay dying at 56 Green Street in the opening of 1845, he answered Monckton Milnes as to the night he had passed: "Oh, horrid, horrid, my dear fellow! I dreamed I was chained to a rock and being talked to death by Harriet Martineau and Macaulay."

Dickens (1812–1870) lived at 48 Doughty Street from 1837 till the end of 1839. Here he wrote the second half of *Pickwick Papers*, the whole of *Oliver Twist* and *Nicholas Nickleby*, and may have begun *Barnaby Rudge*. Among minor work, he edited the *Memoirs of Grimaldi*.

There is no particular reason why this, out of other Dickens' residences, should have been chosen as a museum, but it was the first London house that he rented, while his marriage was young, and this perhaps gives it a touch of pathos.

Charles Darwin (1809–1882) spent from 1839 till 1842 at 110 Gower

Street. He was here when his magnificent *Geology of the Voyage of the Beagle* was published (he had spent almost five years travelling), and *Coral Reefs* was written here. His grandfather, Erasmus Darwin, the fantastical physician and botanist of Lichfield, who refused to be physician to George III, partly anticipated Lamarck's views on evolution, and thus his grandson's also. Charles Darwin had been at work on the theory of natural selection for twenty-one years, and had delayed to publish a sketch of his main conclusions for fourteen, when in 1858 a memoir was addressed to him by the natural historian Alfred Russel Wallace from Indonesia; here, separately discovered, using different terms, was the essence of his own theory. Lyell and Hooker now persuaded him that it would not be precipitate to read an earlier letter of his own and Wallace's memoir to the Linnean Society.

After this, and in spite of ill-health, Darwin never stopped writing. His two most famous books are *The Origin of Species by means of Natural Selection*, published in 1859, and *The Descent of Man*, published in 1871. Disraeli, it will be remembered, was "on the side of the angels" in resultant controversy. There were those who thought both these fascinating books as wicked as any French novel, and Darwin, despite his warm heart and elevated mind, an agent of the Devil.

The other half of his theory was the struggle for existence and the survival of the fittest. Thus the motive force for evolution in the world of plants and animals was suggested to him by extension of Malthus's dismal theory of that terrifying subject, population.

The separate coincidental discoveries of Darwin and of Wallace (whose *On Miracles and Modern Spiritualism* maintains views unusual in scientists) is no more surprising than the coincidences attendant on the discoveries of printing, spectacles, colliery safety-lamps, spermatozoa, and the differential and integral calculus.

In 1876, when he was twenty-three and working in London on a post-graduate thesis, the Russian prophet Vladimir Soloviev saw a vision of the Divine Wisdom as a woman of surpassing loveliness in the Reading-room of the British Museum.

99 Gower Street, later the office of the *Spectator*, was in 1901 the headquarters of the Order of the Golden Dawn in the Outer, under the auspices of Swami Viva Ananda and Theosopho Provost or Theodore Horos—two Americans named Mr and Mrs Frank Dutton Jackson. They had married in the States in 1898. There was a history of fraud and sudden widowhood behind her; she had dramatic, magnetic eyes;

she was a woman of huge, unnatural bulk, weighing perhaps twenty stone, and by then she was close on fifty. He was only thirty-two or so, frail and of slight build. They appear to have been devoted. No difficulty arose about the Occult College they ran at ninety-nine; nor even, in the first place, from the initiation and other ceremonies around the thrones and lamp-lit altars for the novices and priestesses. These they obtained through advertisements in the matrimonial columns, and all became devoted to both of them in spite of meeting anything but marriage. The phallic rites might never have been discussed in a court of law had not one fond girl had a petulant mood about being robbed of jewellery and money.

Horos wore all fawn-coloured clothes for the trial, including frock-coat and bowler hat. The Swami wore different, flowing, priestess-like garments every day, with gloves and a large scent bottle, and she conducted her own defence with almost incredible adroitness, knowledge and formidability. Poor Horos, said to have claimed to be the Son of God, was comparatively feeble. The doctors would not allow his plea of physical incapacity for seduction and rape; the possibility of psychological incapacity was not discussed. That the Swami, with more of a mother's than a wife's rôle, should grudge him nothing is very credible. Apparently, too, whatever else may have taken place, Horos made use of such artificial aids as are ascribed to the Devil's representative at Witches' Sabbaths.

Certainly not one of the girls was kept against her wish. The initiation oath was intimidating, but their loving letters when away and their voluntary returns suggest that the novel life offered emotional warmth and glamour.

When the case had been on some time it was decided to exclude women from the court. Afterwards, despite all the interest offered to the psychologist and the forensic physician, the case was little discussed in the medical or legal Press. *The Lancet*, for example, found the details "too revolting to relate."

The Swami came for judgement in a low-cut, voluminous white satin robe, its flowing sleeves lined with heliotrope, a dazzling white scarf about her. She heaved herself into the dock. The judge gave her husband a sentence of fourteen years. Perhaps moved by her gallant self-defence in a strange country, he gave her a sentence of seven.

At University College, Gower Street, sits Jeremy Bentham's wired skeleton, dressed in his ordinary clothes. He bestowed his "soft and corruptible parts" for anatomical instruction; the rest to be made into the "auto-ikon"—an idea he recommended for all.

83 Gower Street was the childhood home of John Everett Millais. He was a cherished child, and had altogether a most happy life, with his precocious success, the excitement of the original Pre-Raphaelite Brotherhood, his phase of rebellion, his timely reconciliation to orthodoxy, his worldly success, social as well as professional. He earned his financial success by devoting his considerable talent to pleasing the public. In private life there was no artistic nonsense about him and he prided himself on prowess as a sportsman. He was an excellent fellow and very well liked. Euphemia Chalmers Gray, married to Ruskin till the decree of nullity, made the ideal wife for Sir John Millais. "I've had a good time, my boy, a very good time," he said to Philip Calderon near the end.

At 14 Gordon Street (formerly 27) George Meredith (1828–1909) used often to stay, when he visited London, with his great friend Joseph Hardman. They wrote each other joke verses on many an occasion, and used nicknames; Meredith was Robin, Hardman Friar Tuck or just Tucky, and Hardman's wife Mary Ann was Demitroia because, Meredith explained, it had taken a five years' siege to win her. 14 Gordon Street was a friendly, robust, intellectually bustling house where a pioneer party took place in the early sixties—a dinner-party with ladies present at which the men smoked and no one dressed for dinner.

John Ruskin (1819–1900), that great and preposterous man, was born at 54 Hunter Street, now called Ruskin House. He was a prophet of immense honour in his own time and country; yet nothing was learnt from his social vision; his splendid pearls were scattered before swine. Today we have another vexing situation: more people care to read about his private life than to read anything whatever that he has written.

From childhood he had a visual and nervous power of perception that suggests we have most of us a skin too many; though the anguish of his closing years implies that he had a skin too few—not in the sense of "thin-skinned", "touchy", but as one houseless in the world's storm.

He could command a charming, teasing style with the ladies when he liked them. Here is a nice little letter written from Denmark Hill, S.E., to Jean Ingelow, poet and prose writer, in 1869, when they were both around fifty years old,

'Dear Miss Ingelow,

"It is lovely you being so foiled by the sense of my far away Contradictory Spirit.

"So true, and nice, and right of you.

"Can you and your brother come this day week? six o'clock?

"Ever affectionately yours

"J. Ruskin."

In Tavistock House, Tavistock Square, Dickens wrote *Bleak House*, *Hard Times*, and *Little Dorrit*, besides the story called *Hunted Down* for which an American editor paid him £1,000. Here Dickens, Wilkie Collins, Mark Lemon and other intimates acted Wilkie Collins' play *The Lighthouse*, for which Clarkson Stanfield painted the scenery. Dickens bought up a conjuror's whole stock-in-trade one Christmas. and Stanfield was his stooge, imperturbably doing everything wrong to everyone's satisfaction. The premises of the British Medical Association cover the site today.

William Charles Macready, "the eminent tragedian" as he liked to call himself, was born in 1793, lived till 1873, and at one time resided at 45 Stanhope Street, St Pancras. He was the successor to Edmund Kean's glory, though first the old lion was revenged on the young one when they played Othello and Iago as a duel at Drury Lane Theatre in 1832. Little Kean, ruined by gout and drink, pulled himself together to use every trick of "gamesmanship" and outsmart the tall young man.

Macready was forty-eight and at the head of his profession when he took over the management of Drury Lane, 1841–1843. Unofficial scenes which one would like to have heard were the storms between Browning and the eminent tragedian over *The Blot on the 'Scutcheon*. Browning was furious at the cuts and alterations imposed; Macready thought the poet intolerably conceited and the play so bad that he refused to act in it. He had to learn the part after all because Samuel Phelps, the finest actor in his company, was ill at almost the last moment. Phelps went through with it, however, and scored a personal triumph. But *The Blot* only played three times.

Samuel Phelps lived in Islington at 8 Canonbury Square.

Charles Lamb's "cottage in Colebrook Row, Islington" which he liked so well is now 64 Duncan Terrace. It is somewhat altered, no longer detached, less rustic in setting. The New River which ran nearby has been buried. Lamb's absent-minded, eccentric friend

George Dyer walked straight into "the stream Dyerian" in broad daylight, and was presently singing in bed at Colebrook Cottage, having been given too much brandy by the doctor.

Thomas Paine wrote part of his *Rights of Man* at the old Angel Inn, Islington.

Camden Town is a Dickens area. He lived at 16 Bayham Street when he was ten and at 29 (now 13) Johnson Street between the ages of twelve and sixteen. He went to school at the Wellington House Academy in Hampstead Road at Granby Street; it is believed to be Dr Creakle's school.

Towards Kentish Town is Maitland Park Road. Karl Marx lived at 41 from 1875 till his death in 1883. He first settled in London in 1849 at the age of thirty-one. His famous book got by the Russian censor because they found it too dull to read.

In Kentish Town is 39 Hilldrop Crescent, off the Camden Road, which Mrs Crippen decorated in pink as being a lucky colour; she allowed no green. What she said went; she chose her husband's ties and the pattern of his clothes and did all the talking to his tailor. Apparently the doctor didn't mind.

She was his second wife and it had been a love match, when she was seventeen and the mistress of another man in New York, under the name of Cora Turner—reasonably, as her real name was Kunigunde Mackamotzki. Her father was a Russian Pole, her mother a German. Doctor Hawley Harvey Crippen came originally from Coldwater, Michigan.

She was a plump, lively, pretty brunette, with stage ambitions. He paid for her training for grand opera; when they came to England in 1900 he paid for a dazzling range of dresses for music-hall. The agents were obliging, the husband a pattern of indulgence, but she just had no smallest scrap of talent; the stage name of Belle Elmore, the expensive dresses, some Bohemian acquaintances and a restless irritation were all she ever got from her stage endeavours. Her husband was consistently kind and sympathetic in all the disappointments.

They settled in Hilldrop Crescent in 1905. A friend and neighbour, Mrs Harrison, has provided a full description of the Crippens' life there. She scrimped pennies, scattered pounds. She held the purse strings, and when he was providing very well for her started taking in boarders for company, making her husband get up at 6 a.m. to work for them and spending all the money on personal adornment. The boarders, however, were only a passing phase. Her temper got more shrewish and

Dr Crippen

she often chided him for nothing. He was still very fond of her and loved to shower presents on her, especially in public, and especially jewellery; but his quiet, lady-like, methodical typist, Ethel Le Neve, was gaining on his affections. Cora Crippen was methodical in nothing, though she would run the house herself and refused to have a servant. She disliked open windows and fresh air, and did not care for cleaning. The kitchen, where they chiefly lived, was dirty, disordered, and smelly from lack of ventilation. The two cats were imprisoned there to guard their morals, except for occasional airings in a cage in the garden. Mrs Harrison describes the grimy closed windows on a damp, hot day: a litter of dirty crockery, edibles, false curls, brushes, the doctor's collars; a lovely white chiffon gown, embroidered with silk flowers and mounted over white glacé, thrown across a chair; and the female cat scrabbling wildly at the window.

Expenses began to increase. Cora Crippen became a member of the Music Hall Ladies Guild—a charitable society which appealed to her impulsive kindness, made her acquainted with several well-known music-hall people, and so entailed hospitality and further keeping up of appearances. Meanwhile the doctor's great and growing devotion to Miss Le Neve excited his desire to adorn her as he had his wife.

Miss Le Neve had been his mistress for some considerable time when in 1910 he killed his wife with hyoscin. Why then the sudden, rash expedient of murder?

Sir Edward Marshall Hall believed that Cora Crippen was sexually importunate and indeed relentless; that the poor, frail little man, devoted to his mistress, was not equal to these demands; that he knew hyoscin was sometimes used as a sexual depressant in cases of acute nymphomania, but did not know the right dose. But they occupied separate rooms, and there is no known method of enforcing a wife's conjugal rights. Moreover, the mistake in the dose was a very wild one and he left no remnant of the drug for a second occasion.

Cora Crippen had spoken more than once to a friend of leaving her husband taking her money with her, if he would not break his liaison. There was often more money than Crippen's earnings explain. The bulk of it was held in a joint account, and some in the name of Belle Elmore. Perhaps she had earned it herself in the form of presents. She may have threatened him with flight as an ill-used victim to another man's protection, taking all the money and all the shining stones which so delighted him and which he longed to see on his love. She was a woman to feel entitled to all she could get, whether hers or his.

He was considerate as ever in his method of murder. Disposing of the corpse was indeed a grisly business, but he never showed any disturbance at what he had done. Nor did he show concern for himself after his arrest; all his thoughts till the end were for Miss Le Neve. No one who ever met him reported him as other than a kind, unselfish man.

George Joseph Brides-in-the-Bath Smith (whose last murder was committed in Highgate) was quite a contrast—odious, ferocious and fanatically mean.

He had some affection, one presumes, for Miss Edith Pegler, to whom he always returned between bouts with other brides. He hardly ever sent her any money when he was away. Once he sent her £2 in five months and he gave her a portion of Alice Reavil's small trousseau (Miss Reavil had had to pay for all their food). He denied a shilling taxi fare to a bride whom he robbed of her entire £340. Her wedding jaunt was to the National Gallery because it was free, and he left her there on pretext of going to the lavatory while he rushed back to their lodging and stole her clothes. (Perhaps the Gallery suggested his explanation of sudden solvency to his Edith Pegler; he said he had had a lucky deal with a seascape by Turner.) He beat down the price of the bath in which he drowned Miss Mundy and then sent it back unpaid for after it had earned him £2,500. He sold her clothes before they were back from the laundry and stuck his landlady with the laundry bill. It goes on and on. He was arrested, and he was hanged, in a suit he had not stooped to pay for. It was never necessary for him to make a pretence of generosity even during courtship.

Petty, grinding meanness is scarcely glamorous. He was blatant too in demanding to see the bank-books and savings-books of his chosen and in coaching them in curious lies. Poor, uneducated, unprepossessing, he dominated at least ten devoted women between his birth in 1872 at 92 Roman Road, Bethnal Green, and his sudden death in 1915. Of the ten, he married all but the first. Number two, his only real wife, he wedded under the alias George Love. These earliest two he set to steal for him; the others, except for Miss Pegler, he plundered. He murdered three out of the last four. What he had to offer was immense virility and marked attentions. He chose respectable, provincial young women leading rather lonely or dreary lives, aware of emotional need to love and be loved, probably passionate without knowing it. They believed him good and loved him because they wished it so; and afterwards he could make them jump through any hoops, since his highly developed sexuality gave him awareness enough to pick suitable specimens for what was literally his business. In a great number of women he aroused instant dislike and suspicion. Men noticed nothing particular about him at all.

As it is often said that everyone has in them the possibility of writing one interesting book, so is it sometimes said that anyone might commit a murder. This is merely to say that murder can stem from any one of the human passions, and that it is for the most part an amateur crime, Of all professional murderers, Smith was perhaps the most professional, approaching it not as a new departure or desperate solution, but as a mere development of his ordinary occupation. Smith was something of a sadist, but business was little more than business.

Miss Margaret Lofty was thirty-eight, the daughter of a deceased clergyman, doomed to be companion to quiet ladies, disturbed by a disappointment over a married man. When she had insured her life for £700 he married her as John Lloyd on the 17th December 1914—at Bath, as it happened—and took her immediately to Highgate. He had booked rooms in person at 16 Orchard Road, but had made so sinister an impression, especially when speaking of the bath, that the landladies actually called in a detective to refuse him admittance. After some unpleasantness he took poor Peggy Lofty to 14 Bismarck Road, now Waterloo Road. He dragged her to see a doctor, as was his custom, to establish his care and the bride's feebleness—Doctor Bates, 30 Archway Road. She was really unwell, running a temperature of 101°, and there was much for her to do on the morrow; a will to make with Mr Lewis, 84 High Street, Islington; her savings of £19 9*s* 5*d*. to draw from the Muswell Hill Post Office. Therefore she was spared for her bridal night, her last night alive. On 18th December she came back, tired from her errands, to the pleasant domesticity of husband and fireside. At 7.30 p.m. she asked for a warm bath. Already it seemed natural for her husband to come; there was no protest; perhaps his arms around her were very welcome and comforting. She must have got her head from under the water once, for Miss Blatch the landlady heard a sigh—heard a splash, a flop of wet arms on the side of the bath, and that sad last sigh. Then Smith slipped down to play nonchalantly on the parlour organ, out to buy tomatoes, back to be heard ringing on the bell, in to call loudly, pleasantly to the dead.

Among symbols of terror in life is to call unanswered, the voice pursuing a figure that will not turn, the cry in a place deserted by everything save echo. Smith risked a different nightmare. What if dead Miss Lofty had shouted back?

Miss Pegler only once knew him to take a bath himself in all their years together. Several times he cautioned her against them.

In 1816 S. T. Coleridge, who was once almost apprenticed to a cobbler, went to live at the age of forty-four with Doctor and Mrs James Gillman in their hospitable and beautiful house 3 The Grove, Hampstead, until his death eighteen years later. Here he mastered the opium habit to some reasonable extent and became the oracle of a circle of admirers.

Few have been better supplied with benefactors than Coleridge. Beginning with his own brothers, who in 1794 bought him out of the 16th Dragoons, in which he had enlisted the previous year as Silas Tomkyn Comberback, he went on to be the benefactee of, among others, the Bristol publisher Joseph Cottle, a Mr Thomas Poole, the Brothers Wedgwood, the Beaumonts, Wordsworth, De Quincey and Southey. Coleridge, Southey and Robert Lovell had married the three Fricker sisters and planned to found an ideal state on the banks of the Susquehanna. Southey (expelled from Westminster School for an article against flogging and author of the story of *The Three Bears*) presently found himself supporting all three women and their children.

Like De Quincey, Coleridge was driven to drugs by pain: a victim of rheumatism and neuralgia. He was a slave to opium by 1803 and a slave beyond concealment within ten years; though he was fighting it valiantly, with the aid of moderate indulgence in British white wine, around the time his play *Remorse* was produced at Drury Lane in January 1813. It was the best of a bad series of plays then, and ran twenty nights.

Coleridge did his best work on laudanum (opium dissolved in alcohol) which he began to take in 1795, the year of his shiftless marriage. *The Ancient Mariner*, *Kubla Khan*, and the first part of *Christabel* were all written in 1797 and the second part of *Christabel* in 1800. In *The Ancient Mariner* the line on the albatross, "It ate the food it ne'er had ate," is by Wordsworth. Coleridge's original line was more concrete: "The sailors gave it biscuit worms."

In Hampstead, Lord Erskine, with his two leeches and other pets, lived in his retirement by the Spaniards Inn.

Hall Caine (1853–1931), who in his youth bore much of the burden of Rossetti's last two years, and who became a best-seller, lived next door to the Spaniards at Heath End House.

Pitt's House is near the old Bull and Bush; here Chatham retired in nervous melancholia, and had a service hatch made to avoid as far as possible seeing any human being.

Leigh Hunt, that courageous liberal, loved Hampstead, and admired the Heath as much as Constable did, as much as Defoe despised it. He was living in a cottage at West End, Hampstead, at the time of the case against him for libelling the Prince Regent in *Examiner*. There, in 1813, he put on his best suit and chose a little book to carry for the occasion of his sentence, and from there he went to prison. He had his wife and children with him, and "not very providently" did up a room. "I papered the walls with a trellis of roses; I had the ceiling coloured with clouds and sky; the barred windows I screened with Venetian blinds; and when my bookcases were set up with their busts, and flowers and a pianoforte made their appearance, perhaps there was not a handsomer room on that side the water.' And he describes too how he made a little yard into a garden. Charles Lamb was regularly in and out, and among other visitors were Jeremy Bentham (who played battledore and shuttlecock with Hunt), James Mill, Hazlitt, Maria Edgworth, the artist Haydon, Brougham, Byron and Tom Moore. Throughout the two years' sentence (there was also a £500 fine) he continued to edit *Examiner*.

Leigh Hunt's cottage in the Vale of Health has been pulled down, though this little pocket of houses on the Heath is sufficiently intimate-looking to serve in its entirety as a commemoration. He entertained Shelley at Hampstead, and introduced him to Keats, and both to the public in *Examiner*, in 1816.

It is well known that he had no grasp of money matters and that muddle and misery resulted. But in his attitude to money there was more of nobility than of laziness and self-indulgence; his own generosity was given free, without thought of appreciation or return; he did not expect worse from others; nor did he always fail to return loans, or accept whatever was offered.

John Galsworthy lived at Grove House, Hampstead, from 1918 till his death in 1933, and there wrote the greater part of the *Forsyte Saga*.

New Grove House, the Grove, is the house where Svengali was conceived and brought to birth, one of the most vital and memorable of fictional characters, ranking in that respect with Sherlock Holmes. George du Maurier wrote all his three novels in this house, where he lived from 1874, when he was forty, till 1895, the year before his death.

The poet and playwright Joanna Baillie lived in Church Row and afterwards at Bolton House, Windmill Hill. Kemble and Mrs Siddons starred in her *de Montford* at Drury Lane in 1800; *The Family Legend* was also a great success. Byron said she was the only woman who could write tragedy, Sir Walter Scott that she produced "something like a renewal of Shakespeare's inspired strain." Wordsworth praised her as a model English gentlewoman whom he would be pleased to point out to any foreigner.

Romney's house is lower, on Hollybush Hill. He married Mary Abbot when he was twenty-two, and at twenty-eight, with no plan of desertion, left her with their two children at Kendal and set out for London. He heard the dictum of Reynolds that "marriage spoils an artist" (Reynolds, or so he thought, treated him with hostility), and London and foreign travel and new friends and success provided distractions enough to keep him from her for some thirty-six years. For twenty-two of them he lived at 32 Cavendish Square; he made good money; he painted Lady Hamilton in at least thirty characters. He was at the height of his fame, but declining in life, when he retired to Hampstead and the beef-steak dinners with his friends. Weakness of body and mind increased. The end of a poem by Charles Kingsley might have been written for him,

> Creep home and take your place there
> The old and maimed among;
> God grant you find one face there
> You loved when all was young.

"Old, nearly mad, and quite desolate," as Fitzgerald wrote, he went back to his wife, and she welcomed him and cherished him for those last few years till his death in 1802.

Fitzgerald thought her devotion worth all his pictures, even as art, and Tennyson in *Romney's Remorse* makes the painter say:

> O yes, I hope, or fancy that, perhaps,
> Human forgiveness touches heaven and thence—
> For you forgive me, you are sure of that—
> Reflected, sends a light on the forgiven.

Clarkson Stanfield, the friend of Dickens, lived at the corner of Prince Arthur Road and High Street; his house is now the excellent Hampstead subscription library. He became an R.A., but was best known for his remarkable scene painting for the theatre.

John Constable wrote in a letter from 2 Lower Terrace, just near the heath, "I now fear (for my family's sake) I shall never make a popular artist, a gentleman and ladies' painter. But I am spared making a fool of myself." After a few years desertion to Charlotte Street he returned to Hampstead in 1826; briefly to 25 Downshire Hill (since rebuilt), permanently to 40 Well Walk, where he died in 1837.

Rossetti began married life in Downshire Hill, at Spring Cottage (the number is uncertain), because the air was healthier than in his crib on the river. But here too Lizzie was constantly ill and he spent a harassed and harried honeymoon. Within a few months they were back in Blackfriars.

Off Downshire Hill runs Keats Grove, which was named John Street when Keats and his friend Brown lived in one of the two houses collectively called Wentworth Place, and, in the absence of the Dilkes, the Brawnes lived in the other. It was not his first Hampstead lodging; he went there after the death of his brother Tom, with whom he had lived at 1 Well Walk. At Wentworth Place in 1819, already sick, already in love—and loved in return, yet torturing himself, seeing the beloved almost every day—he had his great flowering of poetry. *The Eve of St Agnes*, *The Eve of St Mark*, *La Belle Dame Sans Merci*, the *Ode to Psyche*, the *Ode to a Grecian Urn*, the *Ode to a Nightingale*, *Lamia*, the *Ode to Autumn*, and the greater part of *The Fall of Hyperion* were written there. And there he wrote in a letter to his brother and sister-in-law George and Georgiana in America: "I will call the *world* a School instituted for the purpose of teaching little children to read—I will call the *human heart* the *horn Book* used in that School—and I will call the *Child able to read, the Soul* made from that *School* and its *horn-book*. Do you not see how necessary a World of Pains and troubles is to school an Intelligence and make it a Soul?"

The pretty house is a Museum, its anguish exorcised, its fun and nonsense fled. For of course there was nonsense. "Brown," once reported Keats, "has been walking up and down the room breeding, now at this moment he is being delivered of a couplet—and I daresay will be as well as can be expected—Gracious—he has twins!"

I do not know where in Hampstead was or is Woodbine Cottage. The evangelist Mrs Thistlethwayte, once the demi-mondaine Laura Bell, settled there in 1887 after the death of her husband. She was the centre of an eminent, staid and select circle, including Mr and Mrs Gladstone. She was much in Gladstone's confidence. He made a special visit to tell her of his resignation from the Premiership before putting it in the hands of the Queen, and after her death in 1894 her letters from him were found to fill a large box.

Laura Bell was to the fifties what Skittles was to the sixties. The equestrian style was already established. From Glenconway, Co. Antrim, she went to be a shop-girl in Belfast, but was soon established in Dublin with her barouche and pair of white horses. She came to London, Wilton Crescent, in 1850. Sir F. C. Burnand writes in *Records & Reminiscences*:

"As a 'boy about town' I remember several notorious Hetæræ being pointed out to me, as they rode in spanking style in the Row, were driven in open landaus, or charioteered themselves about Hyde Park in the season. . . . Clearly do I call to mind Laura Bell's pretty, doll-like face, her big eyes, not ignorant of an artistic touch that added a lustre to their natural brilliancy, and her quiet vivacious glances as she sat in an open phaeton, vivaciously talking with a variety of men, all 'swells' of the period, of course, at the corner of the drive near the Achilles statue, while her smart little 'tiger' stood at the horses' heads. What strange stories I used to hear of her recklessness, her prodigality, her luxury, and her cleverness! Was not her liaison with the chief of the Nepaulese princes, Jung Bahadoor, who alone was a temporary fortune to her, the theme of songs of the period?"

The story that she won Hyderabad to the English cause in the mutiny of 1857 by getting the Prince of Wales's help in sending her old love a ring he had given with a promise, and that Edward "never failed to show what gratitude he could to the lady who had put her reputation at the service of her country," is suspect when one recalls that the English prince was scarcely sixteen at that time and under very strict surveillance.

She was at the height of her notoriety, everyone standing to see her arrival at the opera, when she married Augustus Charles Thistlethwayte in 1852. It was not particularly successful. Her extravagance was deplorable, and he more than once gave public notice that he would not be responsible for her debts.

In the autumn of 1862, beautifully dressed, a black mantilla over her golden hair, magnificent jewels round her neck, diamonds on her hands, she was holding revivalist meetings in the mountains of Ross-shire. Tones of impassioned conviction and emotion, remnants of great beauty, generosity to the poor, made many converts. So great was her repentance and spiritual gifts that some of the aristocracy received her, and she won gradual acceptance from the county. As late as 1874, when she preached to packed houses at the Polytechnic, Sir Willoughby

Laura Bell

Maycock was much impressed by the lustre of her eyes. She was painted three times; Girard's portrait went to the Wallace Collection.

The great Thomas Henry Huxley (1825–1895) moved into 4 Marlborough Place, St John's Wood, "amid endless rain and mud" in December 1872. He kept this address till 1890. He had the quick wit which one thinks of as something quite separated from powerful intellectual development, but which often goes with it. One of his students complained of being always unable to remember in which side of the heart was the tricuspid and in which the mitral valve. "It's easy to remember which is the mitral valve," said Huxley; "a bishop couldn't be in the right." On another occasion someone was speaking to the Linnaean or some other learned society on the question of whether or not acquired characteristics could be transmitted. He pointed out that mutilation was never inherited, and instanced circumcision being performed anew from generation to generation. Whereupon T. H. Huxley was heard to murmur:

> "There's a divinity that shapes our ends,
> Rough-hew them how we will."

George Eliot lived in St John's Wood from 1864 till 1880; G. H. Lewes died in 1878. Their house, 21 North Bank, has been swept away by railroad construction.

Elm Park Mansions now stands where Mr and Mrs Thomas Hood once lodged at 17 Elms Row, St John's Wood, and where he wrote for the Christmas number of *Punch*, 1843, *The Song of the Shirt*, which fairly rocked the public. His last house, where he died in 1845, was Devonshire Lodge, Finchley Road, next to the present Marlborough Road Station of the Metropolitan Railway. Hood was frolicsome and gentle and neat at puns, like his friend Lamb. Ill-health and poverty made his a life of hardship; he had to keep working even on his death-bed ("But things may take a turn, as the pig said on the spit.") One of his last poems was the memorable *Bridge of Sighs*. But it could not be called an unhappy life. He had natural gaiety, was liked, and was congenially, devotedly married. ("Hood, Hood, how can you run on so?" she used to say indulgently, as he rattled along, or sang some song of his own, such as "If you go to France, be sure you learn the lingo.") Sir Robert Peel settled a pension of £100 on Mrs Hood before her husband died.

At 17 Hanover Terrace, Regent's Park, lived that delightful and astringent man of letters Edmund Gosse.

The borough of St Marylebone is rich in associations. Boswell died where today stands 102 Great Portland Street. Lord Lister of the antiseptic system lived at 12 Park Crescent.

Romney's house at 32 Cavendish Square has already been mentioned. Here too Lady Mary Wortley Montagu had a house, and so had the famous Lady Bessborough. When her jewels were stolen from it, Lady

Bessborough was in great distress for fear that the thieves should be traced, and of course hanged.

Byron was born at 16a Holles Street, Cavendish Square. It was pulled down, but a bust of Byron was placed on 24 Holles Street, raised on the same site, and was destroyed by the blitz.

Gladstone at one time lived at 73 Harley Street, the greatest of the great Victorian statesmen.

At 2 Devonshire Place Conan Doyle had a consulting-room and nothing to do. He would walk from his lodging in Montagu Place, arrive at ten and wait till three or four. Here Sherlock Holmes, already the hero of two little books, really came into his own. Conan Doyle began the famous series of short stories for the *Strand Magazine*, afterwards published as *The Memoires* and *The Adventures* of Sherlock Holmes. Here Doctor Watson was groomed for a household word, and brilliant brother Mycroft Holmes was born.

At 82 Wimpole Street died Wilkie Collins, who created one of the best villains in literature with Count Fosco of *The Woman in White*.

The most famous number in Wimpole Street is 50; there lived the Barretts. There Browning engaged himself to Elizabeth Barrett before he knew that she could stand. He said it was the greatest surprise of his life when his betrothed rose to greet him.

Henry Hallam the historian moved to 67 Wimpole Street in 1819 when his son Arthur was eight years old, and stayed till 1840. There Tennyson came to visit the young friend upon whose death he was to write *In Memoriam*. He wrote of "the long unlovely street," and Miss Barrett of walls like "Newgate's turned inside out."

At 14 York Place (now 120 Baker Street) lived the younger Pitt whose final death-bed words were perhaps the most brave and reckless ever recorded: "I think I could fancy one of Bellamy's mutton pies."

Michael Faraday, the blacksmith's son (1791–1867), resided at one time at 48 Blandford Street. Sir Humphrey Davy found the young chemist and natural philosopher working for a bookbinder, engaged him as assistant, and took him as his amanuensis on a Continental tour. Lady Davy treated him as a menial.

Wilkie Collins lived for a long time at what was then 90 Gloucester Place, but has since been renumbered. The house is a little south of Dorset Street, but hard to identify.

At 39 Montagu Square, Anthony Trollope wrote the finest specimen of his late, cynical style, *The Way We Live Now*. *The Prime Minister* (1876), *The American Senator* (the next year) and *Is he Popenjoy?* (the year after) are also among his very good books. *South Africa* and *John Caldigate* were written here, and the *Autobiography* was at least begun. It is certainly a house to reverence.

Of houses to reverence, 1 Devonshire Terrace, Marylebone Road, is notable—and probably to be demolished. Dickens lived there from 1839 to 1851, and wrote *The Old Curiosity Shop, Barnaby Rudge, Martin Chuzzlewit, Dombey & Son, A Christmas Carol, The Cricket on the Hearth, The Battle of Life,* and *David Copperfield.*

V

West; Paddington, Kensington, Fulham, etcetera

Our journey west starts from Marble Arch, or rather from the south-east corner of Connaught Square, where stood "Tyburn's Triple Tree"—a triangular gallows with three legs to stand on; the "three wooden stilts" of Rawbone's flight of fancy in Shirley's play *The Wedding*.

Derrick, the hangman in Shakespeare's day, gave that name to a temporary crane formed on board ship with one spar lashed to another gibbet fashion, used for general purposes of hoisting. Dekker took his name in vain several times: "For he rides his circuit with the devil, and Derrick must be his host, and Tiburne the land at which he will light."

Jack Ketch, operating in the time of Judge Jeffreys, was a most barbarous wretch, who did not shrink from botching the job. His name endured as a nickname for his successors.

Taylor, the Water Poet, wrote in 1623:

> I have heard sundry men of times dispute
> Of trees that in one yeare will twice bear fruit;
> But if a man note Tyburn, 'twill appeare
> That that's a tree that bears twelve times a yeare.

Here in the reign of James I was hanged Mrs Turner, the poisoner, a woman with the remains of great beauty, who had much influenced fashion at Court and was the inventor of yellow starch. John Timbs alleges that Lord Chief Justice Coke sentenced her to be hanged in yellow-starched ruffs and cuffs, hoping that the inventor of "that horrid garb . . . would be the last by whom they would be worn." There is a good deal of evidence that the hangman was wag enough to wear big cuffs and a ruff in the no-longer-to-be-popular colour, and that there was a large audience for his drollery, including ladies as well as gentlemen of quality. Mrs Turner was rouged and dressed with great care for her last appearance. She made a most penitent end.

Mrs Turner and Frances Howard, Countess of Somerset, joined to inflict a most vile and desolate death in a prolonged serial of agony upon Sir Thomas Overbury, from love. The young, dazzling Frances was blinded and calloused in her passion for Robert Carr to all but her own urgency; it was enough that Overbury opposed the match. And Mrs Turner was genuinely devoted to Frances, though glad no doubt of such a grateful and powerful patroness. She never foresaw any limit to that power and was amazed at her own calamity. "O, my Lady Somerset," she cried in prison, "woe worth the time that I ever knew her!" But she always said that she loved her dearly. Lady Somerset had grown reciprocally attached to her over the debilitating powders for her first husband to preserve her honour from him, the aphrodisiacs for her second, the black magic, the wax images and the leaden, and the rose algar, white arsenic, acqua fortis and powdered diamonds.

Mrs Turner was hanged in 1615. The Countess was reprieved and survived her by seventeen years, but for a grimmer destiny.

There is disagreement as to whether Lord Ferrers was or was not hanged with a silken rope, but he was the first to try a new kind of drop. When his estates were ruined by his dissipation, the Court of Chancery ordered that rents due to him should be given direct to a paid receiver, whom he might nominate. He thought his faithful steward would prove a pliant tool, and found he did not. The situation had every possibility for misunderstanding and offence. The Earl came to hate the man, brooded on a "just" revenge, and sickened of his purpose too late, yet before it was quite accomplished. He drove to Tyburn in his own landau and six, wearing his wedding clothes, and was as cool and as stylish as any highwayman.

Highwaymen were the aristocracy of scoundrels, much admired by women. John Rann, "Sixteen-string Jack," was a highwayman famous for foppery in dress. The sixteen strings were said to represent sixteen trials and acquittals; Boswell tells us he wore them bunched at the knees of his breeches. He wore a pea-green coat to Tyburn and carried a huge nosegay handed him (a usual practice) by a prostitute from the steps of St Sepulchre's.

Claud Duval, another to die at Tyburn, was captain of a gang especially active in Holloway, where Devil's Lane was renamed Duval's Lane. Macaulay's *History of England* says: "It is related how at the head of his troop he stopped a lady's coach in which there was a booty of £400; how he took only one hundred, and suffered the fair owner to ransom the rest by dancing a coranto with him on the heath." Frith, when painting a picture of this scene, was exercised to find out how one dances the coranto.

The fashionable James Maclaine, the Gentleman Highwayman, came of honourable stock. How his spirited Irish confederate, Plunkett, ever put up with such a partner, how any glamour could attach to so consistent a coward and shirker as Mr Maclaine turned out to be, is an enigma. He was really a pitiful fellow. Yet his friend must have got quite attached to him and the ladies doted.

Plunkett lodged in Jermyn Street, Maclaine in St James's Street, with a country hide-out in Chelsea. There he repaid a loan to a mistress, and had Plunkett hold her up for it on her way home. The only shot he ever fired was by mistake, when he held up Horace Walpole coming back from Holland House; Walpole's face was scorched and the ball passed through the roof of his coach. Mr Maclaine wrote him two letters of apology for the robbery and the accident.

When Maclaine was arrested in 1750 through a piece of slip-shod folly, the most prominent of many comforters were Lady Caroline Petersham, afterwards Countess of Harrington, and Miss Ashe. Horace Walpole called them Polly and Lucy and asked them if their protégé did not sing, like Gay's Macheath, "Thus I stand like the Turk with his doxies around." This though the Gentleman Highwayman whined and wept in court and offered to betray Plunkett. In one of the many prints published of Mr Maclaine he is shown supported by the two ladies. A very pretty lady had been found at his lodging too, superintending his many rich suits of clothes and thirty-three stolen purses.

Mr John Thrift, who was hangman at the time, but had been lying perdu because of a quite private and unauthorised execution, returned to public life for Maclaine's arrival at Tyburn.

Doctor Colenso, first Bishop of Natal, stayed for a while at 23 Sussex Place while hullabaloo raged about him in the 1860's. He had soon mastered the Zulu language, prepared a grammar and dictionary, translated the Prayer Book and part of the Bible. He objected to the doctrine of eternal punishment, declined to tell enquiring coloured people that he literally believed the Noah's Ark story, and thought it unjust to order converted Zulu chiefs to discard all but one of the wives they had already married. In 1862 came out the first book of his seven-volume critical examination of the Pentateuch and the Book of Joshua. Mild and scholarly though it seems, it was a sensation. Both Houses of Convocation condemned it. The laity made jokes and puns: "Have you heard Colenso's mad? He's already given his pen to Tuke"—Tuke being a famous alienist of the day.

In 1861 speculation about his "Pentateuch" was already sufficient to embarrass John Murray, who had the bad luck to have undertaken a Biblical Dictionary, to be edited by Doctor W. Smith with various contributors. Volume one cleverly gained a respite: "Ark—see Flood." Farrar, later Archdeacon of Westminster and Dean of Canterbury, was commissioned for the Flood article. They paid him; but was it a little free and unorthodox? Better play for time again. It appeared as "Flood—see Noah."

After his wife's death in 1861, Robert Browning settled at 19 Warwick Crescent, with his father, his sister, his only son, and his son's white owl, which was petted and respected by them all. He stayed for over a quarter of a century, and wrote *Dramatis Personae, The Ring and the Book*, and all other poetry of his second period, except his last volume. A plaque marks the house, as suggested by the late Sir Edmund Gosse—"One of those graceful and unobtrusive roundels." The canal gives charm to the district. Young Pen Browning used to row upon it and sometimes skate, and Robert Browning would point out the bridge to which Byron dragged John Murray to show him where a publisher had drowned himself.

Browning told Rossetti once that his Italian valet was interested in famous Englishmen, so that after a visit from Thackeray he explained to him that that was one of our most distinguished authors. "Ah! Signor Murray!" cried the valet reverently, remembering the famous handbooks so inseparable from all the English abroad.

Holland House, Holland Park, built in 1607, is named from Henry Rich, Earl of Holland (younger son of the first Earl of Warwick, and Penelope, who was Sir Philip Sidney's Stella). He fought on both sides in the Civil War and the Roundheads beheaded him; he is supposed to walk still, with his head in his hand. John Aubrey, the seventeenth-century antiquary, tells us: "The beautiful Lady Diana Rich, as she was walking in her father's garden at Kensington, to take the fresh air before dinner, about 11 o'clock, being then very well, met with her own apparition, habit and everything, as in a looking-glass. About a month after, she died of the small-pox. And it is said that her sister, the Lady Elizabeth Thynne, saw the like of herself before she died. This account I had from a person of honour."

This was the most notable of noblemen's houses during the Commonwealth, when acting was proscribed, for having actors to perform for small gatherings of nobility and gentry, afterwards making up a sum for them. But it first became really celebrated in the reign of

George I, when Charlotte, widow of Edward Rich, Earl of Warwick and Holland (for his father had become heir to both titles), married Joseph Addison. It is supposed that Addison intended Sir Roger de Coverley's courtship of the widow for a playful description of his own —which was actually tedious and formal, and was originally entertained by the Countess for a laugh. His growing fame as a writer and a political personage (Under-Secretary of State) helped to persuade her to a marriage which proved unhappy. He endured it through resource to the bottle and by entertaining Swift, Pope and other distinguished friends, but died three years later.

After Addison's death, Holland House remained in the possession of the Warwick family and their heir, Lord Kensington, till Henry Fox bought it, and, being raised to the peerage, took his title from his mansion. He was notorious in a corrupt age for the loot he made out of his Government positions. When he was enriching himself as Paymaster of the Forces, there was a great outcry on the badness of the ammunition served out in Admiral Byron's West Indies engagement. Henry Fox fought a duel with a Mr Adam soon after, and being struck but scarcely injured by his adversary's shot, exclaimed: "Egad, sir! It would have been all over with me if we had not charged our pistols with Government powder."

Henry Fox, first Lord Holland, had a happy life. He acquired wealth and didn't care how. He ran away with Lady Georgiana Caroline Lennox (she had staved off a crucial meeting with the family's choice, to their great indignation, by cutting off her eyebrows), and not only did they love each other dearly, but they were soon reconciled to her parents, the Duke and Duchess of Richmond. He was a gay and joyous friend, a devoted and indulgent father. Only when health and spirits declined towards the end was he less perfectly satisfied with his career.

He did not believe in thwarting children. When he found that his younger son, Charles James, positively craved to smash a watch, he said, "Well, if you must, I suppose you must," and supplied one. When the child had been promised to see a wall blown up with gunpowder, but missed the operation, he had the wall rebuilt and blown up again, advising those around never to break promises to children.

George Selwyn, notorious for his love of executions and of being in at the death with his acquaintances, called on him when he was dangerously ill. He said to a servant after, "Be so good, in case Mr Selwyn comes again, to show him up without fail; for if I am alive I shall be delighted to see him, and if I am dead he will be delighted to see me."

His grandson Henry Richard Fox became the third lord in 1774, before he was a year old. He was permanently lamed in childhood and so debarred from exercise; his tastes by good fortune were

Henry Fox, Lord Holland

scholarly and intellectual, a writer and a great reader. In public life he was liberal minded, and he strongly advocated mitigation of the criminal code. He had a gentle, charming, rather happy character. One of his friends wrote, "Nothing was proscribed with him. As of old, the meanest wayfarers used to be received hospitably, lest angels should be turned away; so Lord Holland seemed to have a hearing for every argument, lest a truth should be shut out from his mind."

As a quiet young man of twenty-three he ran away with Lady Webster, who had been dismally married at fifteen to a man much older than herself. She was born Elizabeth Vassall, heiress of an immensely wealthy American family more recently from Jamaica. Her vast vitality was a charm to those who liked her, intolerable to those who did not. She was beautiful, bold and unconventional, loyal, honest and no fool, shrewd, crude, rude and incredibly dominating. They met in 1792. It was four and a half years before the Webster marriage was dissolved and the Holland marriage celebrated. He was then three and twenty and she twenty-six.

The brilliant and generous Devonshire House set were her friends; otherwise, women for the most part cold-shouldered the divorcée. But she had her hands full enough collecting the best male brains of the day. Talleyrand, Byron, Tom Moore, Macaulay, Lord Melbourne, Sheridan, Wilberforce, Sydney Smith, Campbell were some of them. The poet Samuel Rogers was a sort of oracle there, and had his own room, where he often stayed. When Sheridan did so, a servant was told off for all-night attendance in the room next his, to bring him champagne should he wake up thirsting and quench his bed curtains should he set them alight.

Like many people with bullying manners, Lady Holland would accept a little pertness and standing up to. After receiving a few orders, Sydney Smith asked if he should also sweep the floor, and d'Orsay suggested sitting under the dining-room table as the quickest way to keep on picking up her napkin.

At 18 Melbury Road, nearby, lived Holman Hunt. He was once asked a most insufferable question. He had painted, at great expenditure of time, money, spirit, and endurance of hardship, his picture *The Scapegoat*. He brought it back from the Palestine desert and showed it to Gambart, a famous London art-dealer. "What's it doing?" asked Gambart.

Thackeray lived at 13 (now 16) Young Street from 1847 till 1854; and there he wrote his finest and most readable work: *Vanity Fair*, *Pendennis*, and *Esmond*. There too he wrote part of another but less readable favourite, *The Newcomes*, to be finished in his next house, 36 Onslow Square.

Thackeray knew that *Vanity Fair* was his masterpiece. When he was especially congratulated on Becky Sharp's feeling of pride in her husband while he ruined her plans and chances by thrashing Lord Steyne, he answered candidly, "Well, when I wrote that sentence I slapped my fist on the table and said, 'That is a touch of genius!'" Years later, when he had left Young Street but was passing down it with a friend, he cried in mock solemnity, before his old home, "Down on your knees, you rogue, for here *Vanity Fair* was penned, and I will go down with you, for I have a high opinion of that little production myself."

He put a lot of himself into *Pendennis* and thought it something of a self-portrait; when his American friend, Mrs Baxter, protested that Pendennis was so weak, he replied, "Ah, well, Mrs. Baxter, your humble servant is not very strong." A curious episode in Young Street resulted from it. It contains a reference to Catherine Hayes, the grim heroine of his *Catherine*, published a few years earlier, once landlady of The Hog in the Pound, in Argyll Street, W.1, which was nicknamed The Gentleman in Trouble; she suffered death at Tyburn in 1726, having murdered her husband for her paramour's sake and chopped up the body helped by two servants. A young Irish singer, Miss Catherine Hayes, was at the height of her fame when *Pendennis* came out, and a group of young Irishmen decided to come to England in turn till one of them succeeded in avenging the supposed reference to her. Mr Briggs, the first (and, in fact, the last) to arrive, took lodgings opposite Thackeray in Young Street, and sent a letter announcing the coming chastisement. Thackeray walked over to confront him, delivered a quiet little lecture on the murderess, and having appeased the young fire-eater bought a fine Chippendale chair from his landlady.

The Young Street house was Thackeray's first family home since the early years of happy marriage before his wife's madness, for he sent to Paris for the young daughters to whom he was so kind a father.

Nearby is 2 Palace Green, the house he had built in Queen Anne style, where he moved in 1862 and finished *The Adventures of Philip*. He died there the following year.

John Stuart Mill lived at 18 Kensington Square, where he had not just one but several busts of Jeremy Bentham.

Addison lodged in Kensington Square before winning his widow and regretting it at Holland House.

Talleyrand, when in London (1792–1794), moved to Kensington Square from Woodstock Street. Born with a club foot, forced into the church and denied an eldest son's privileges, he was less soured than might have been expected; cynical, indeed, but pleasant tempered and kind to children, besides being a great wit and teller of anecdotes. "After listening to him for an hour," wrote Madame de la Tour du Pin, "one was compelled to banish the recollection of everything one had heard against him. Worthless himself, he hated, strangely enough, what was bad in others. Listening to him without knowing him, one would believe he was virtuous." Years later, in a letter to her sister, Harriet Granville wrote: "It is difficult and painful to believe he is not the very best man in the world, so gentle, so kind, so simple and so grand. One forgets the past life, the present look. I could have sat for hours listening to him." A friend he used to visit was Mary Woolstonecraft, the feminist, who used the same cups at the same meal both for tea and for wine. As a girl she was in love (as when was she not in love, poor lady?) with a botanist who professed himself gratified by her clever company and that of her friend, Fanny Blood, but thought it a pity they did not mend the holes in their stockings.

Henry James lived at 34 De Vere Gardens. As a ten-year-old boy in New York he met Thackeray, who was amused by his tight, brass-buttoned jacket, different from English juvenile wear. It gave young Henry that impression of the oddness of Americans which runs through his novels.

Browning's last home was also in De Vere Gardens. He moved there in 1887, and died in Venice two years later on the publication day of his last book of poems.

W. S. Gilbert, that "source of innocent merriment," lived at 39 Harrington Gardens, south of Kensington High Street.

Still farther south is Finborough Road, not very far from Earls Court underground station, where at number 13a, a basement flat, Ronald True realized a fantasy. There he killed a well-conducted young street-walker, renamed Olive Young, who had previously been a shop girl named Gertrude Yates.

In all True's tall stories of his adventures in remote climes, anyone he had murdered was a man. It was always a man or men—and of course one, or more, who had injured him—with whom he planned a show-down. True was armed with a revolver; he always carried it with him ready loaded, and had filed the noses of the bullets. His imaginary enemy's weapon was also a revolver. This had a kind of logic, for the chief enemy was an externalized self whom he called "the other Ronald True." When he multiplied him by two, he brought in Ronald *Trew*, whom he knew of as a real member of Murray's Club, which he himself had frequented, but whom he had not met. Only

Thackeray

Conan Doyle

William Morris (*right*) with Burne-Jones

Dickens

George du Maurier

John Keats

The young Leigh Hunt

The young Dickens

when there was further multiplication did new names come up, and never to the exclusion of the other Ronald True and the existent but legendized Ronald Trew. Sometimes there was a question whether several enemies were not impersonating him. As True careered about London with his loaded weapon it was himself, or a *doppelganger*, that he sought.

"The other" had been created in one of the many nursing-homes to which his originator had been consigned for treatment of the morphia habit. His function was to carry True's failures, leaving him to shine unclouded as he thought he deserved. When True backed horses from Doctor Parham's home the racing results came to him by telegram. Any telegram announcing a winner he of course accepted as really for him. Telegrams with bad news and all bills were intended for someone else of the same name. As a device to deceive others it couldn't be taken seriously. As a device to deceive himself it preserved the self-satisfaction of a deranged mind unable to adapt itself by sane means and with genuine success to the external world; it was an insane accommodation to environment. As the real Ronald True progressed in thieving and fraud, "the other" changed from an unsuccessful person who happened to have the same name, to a deliberate impersonator who forged cheques which True's mother had to take up; this became the centre of a homicidal dream.

True's prattle, often jocular, on the subject of murder never alarmed his men friends. They took it as part of his tall talk and high spirits, of his being a card, and mad in a merely colloquial sense, which made him amusing company. Women recognized him as genuinely "mad, bad and dangerous to know." Perhaps only women were in danger, so long as he was at large and his violence could choose. His affection for his wife changed to hostility. The only person actually threatened with his famous revolver was a Mrs Wilson, when she refused to go out with him. He had met her at Murray's and taken a possessive fancy to her. She always insisted that his harmless boon-companion Armstrong should accompany them there; and perhaps her life was saved by True's presenting a cheque at Murray's which was cashed by confusion with the genuine member Ronald Trew; for thereafter the club had to be avoided. His pursuit of Olive Young began at once. She refused to make a second appointment though he rang her up continually, and was fortunate in being out every time he came to Finborough Road (in a hired car on credit) from the 19th February 1922 till the night of Sunday, the 5th of March. Then, when she saw who her caller was, she was in a dilemma, not eager to raise an outcry, make trouble in the house or ask protection of the police. She hoped for the best. He slept with her, and next day performed the homely, considerate act of making her an early-morning cup of tea. She did not live to drink it.

In the murder fantasy which True had made so public, the victim was to be an armed man, a criminal who owed him and his mother financial amends, and who was to be killed—failing the amends—with a revolver. The realization was very different. He killed, with a rolling-pin, a helpless girl who had never done him harm; then picked her purse and took her jewellery; there thus appeared a sane motive, for he was penniless and had been living—with curious success—on his scattered wits. But "the other Ronald True" could not be killed, being both non-existent and indispensable. And into the fantasy talk with which he regaled acquaintances he wove the actual realization, and furnished, though they could not then be pieced together, a complete set of scattered clues to what he would do. He revealed that he wanted money from someone in a basement flat at Fulham, that he would get it even if it meant murder, that he had been frustrated over fixing an appointment, but thought he would succeed at the weekend, that Monday's papers would announce the person's murder in that basement flat at Fulham, and that a girl whom he knew called Olive was being cruelly persecuted by another man. Once again "the other" carried his sins.

It is considered unlucky to meet one's *doppelganger*. But one could wish that Ronald True had met his, like poor Lady Diana Rich and Lady Elizabeth Thynne at Holland House in Kensington.

Frail Olive Young (she was only twenty-five) might well walk in Finborough Road, followed by that most insubstantial of all shades, "the other Ronald True."

The Albert Hall has replaced Gore House and its garden. Wilberforce lived there for thirteen years, from 1808 till 1831, and in its library began that agitation which ended in the abolition of West Indian slavery. After him, Lady Blessington held court there. Prince Louis Napoleon was at one of her dinner-parties in August 1840 and puzzled the company by inviting them to dine with him that day twelve month at the Tuileries. It was the evening before his futile swoop on Boulogne, and four days later they knew of his abortive landing and captivity. In 1846, on the first day of his escape to England, he dined with Lady Blessington again; among fellow-diners was Walter Savage Landor and Alfred Count d'Orsay, her handsome lover, who was especially vain of his feet. D'Orsay painted a large picture of Gore House garden, with Lady Blessington and the Duke of Wellington in the right foreground, Landseer in the centre painting a cow and her calf, himself with two favourite dogs on the right, Lord Chesterfield to the left, the two Miss Powers reading a letter, with Lord Brougham, Lord Douro, etcetera, here and there. Other frequent visitors were Dickens and Thackeray, and Tom Moore, whose singing unlocked fountains of tears in drawing-rooms. Despite the fortune her husband left her and all her output of novels, after nineteen years of social brilliance and extravagance Lady Blessington sold home and possessions in 1849, fled with d'Orsay to Paris, and died in crushing debt a few months later. Louis Napoleon was slow to reward the old friendship and support of the bankrupt d'Orsay. The Directorship of Fine Arts in Paris was conferred on him a few days before his death in 1852.

VI

South; Knightsbridge, Chelsea, Lambeth, Whitehall, etcetera

A little west of Wilton Place stood, amidst fields, a handsome mansion called Knightsbridge Grove, with a fine avenue of trees approaching it. In about 1790 it was taken by a "Mrs Smith." Poor Mrs Smith was the notorious Mrs Cornelys, whose disreputable balls and masquerades in Carlisle House, Soho Square, had packed in the world of fashion, and yet had not made her fortune. Her house and furniture had been auctioned in 1785 by decree of the Court of Chancery, but, undaunted, she fitted up her new venture in splendid style. A great suite of rooms was gaudily embellished for those who liked to breakfast in public and to drink fresh asses' milk. But taste and manners were changing; the style, the touch of the once infallible empress of fashion was no longer the mode. She abandoned the scheme and fled her merciless creditors, dying a prisoner for debt in the Fleet Prison on an August day of 1797.

Laura Bell lived in Wilton Crescent, when she first came to London, a young courtesan, driving fashionably in Hyde Park and not dreaming of revivalist meetings to come.

At the corner of Knightsbridge and Wilton Place stood, till 1840, a tobacconist's shop, which encroached much on the thoroughfare. Here lived the old, eccentric Mrs Dowell, who had what we now call a "thing" about the Duke of Wellington. She was so pertinacious with her gifts of patties, cakes and other delicacies that his servants could not stand up to her and took in the parcels. She always laid an extra knife and fork for him at her table in case he should drop in for pot luck . . . one day.

In Sloane Street in 1786 lodged Count Cagliostro, a magician and swindler with a very pretty wife, and believed to be Giuseppe Balsamo from Palermo. There in Sloane Street he wrote his *Letter to the English People*, which was savagely mocked by M. de Morande, the editor of the *Courrier de l'Europe*. Cagliostro answered him in the *Public Advertiser* on 3rd September.

"In physics and chemistry, Mr Joker, arguments go for little and sneers for nothing—experience is all. Permit me, then, to propose a little experiment, which will divert the public, either at your expense or at mine. I invite you to breakfast for the 9th November next, at nine o'clock in the morning; you will furnish the wine and the accessories; I will furnish one dish in my own style—a little sucking pig, fattened according to my method. Two hours before breakfast I will present him to you alive, fat and healthy. You will engage to have him killed and cooked, and I will not go near him till the moment he is put on the table; you shall cut him yourself into four pieces, choose that which attracts you the most, and give me any piece you please. The day after this breakfast one of four things will have happened: either we shall be both dead or both alive or I shall be dead and you alive, or you dead and I alive. Out of these four chances I give you three, and I bet 5,000 guineas that the day after the breakfast you will be dead and I shall be in good health. You will confess that no fairer offer could be made, and that you must either accept the wager or confess your ignorance, and that you have foolishly and dully cut your jokes upon a subject beyond your knowledge."

And M. de Morande was much laughed at, for he dared not accept the wager.

When Oscar Wilde was arrested at the Cadogan Hotel, Sloane Street, he had a yellow-bound copy of *Aphrodite*, by his friend Pierre Louys. "Arrest of Oscar Wilde. Yellow Book under his Arm," said newspaper headlines. This was taken to mean the contemporary periodical *The Yellow Book*, with which he had never had anything to do. At once a mob demonstrated outside the offices of the Bodley Head in Vigo Street, and smashed the windows. "It killed *The Yellow Book*," said its publisher, John Lane, "and it nearly killed me." This is just another of those episodes so evocative of Cinna the poet in *Julius Caesar*.

The maddening thing about the arrest is that Wilde was accused of offences against a section of an Act which had been in force less than ten years, and which was loudly recognized the moment that it was too late as the "Blackmailer's Charter." Into a perfectly good Act for the protection of women and children, Mr Labouchere suddenly introduced a clause creating the new offence of indecency between male persons in public *or private*. This widely condemned contribution of

Algernon Charles Swinburne

Mr Labouchere's helps to explain to us why the adjective "Victorian" is sometimes used opprobriously of an age which produced so staggering a catalogue of great men, and against which so many of them were in revolt.

Algernon Charles Swinburne was born in 1837 in Chapel Street, Belgravia. He grew into a frail, freakish young man, very vain, very brave and very odd-looking. His forehead was huge and bulging, his hair a flaming red, and his face twitched nervously. His friends treated him indulgently, as a sort of *enfant terrible*. At a party of Rossetti's at Blackfriars in 1861 he insisted that the Marquis de Sade was the flower and apostle of perfection, though it soon came out that he had never read a word of him. At that party or another he announced his wish to build seven towers and commit one of the deadly sins in each of them. A fidgetty, twittering figure, unable to drink without being ill, he flung himself gallantly into Bohemian life. He investigated the Hermit's Cave, the Fairy Bower, the Polka-dancing mob at Cremorne, explored the Haymarket resorts and the grim gaieties of the slums. It is said that Rossetti urged him on to make love to the equestrienne poetess Adah Mencken, who made such a hit as Mazeppa at the Astley Theatre. They were photographed together, looking strangely paired. She talked to him of their common interest, but he replied, "Darling, a woman who has such beautiful legs need not discuss poetry." It is a good example of that apartness and selfishness which are two of the difficulties in human communication; Swinburne, sure of his poetry, must have wished to be valued as an attractive male; Adah Mencken, confident of her legs, must have longed to hear her writing appreciated. However, these were not the last words on the subject; Swinburne did praise her poetry, and so did Tennyson.

Sir Francis Chantrey (he was knighted in 1835 at the age of fifty-four) lived in Eccleston Street from shortly after his marriage to a well-to-do cousin in 1807 until his death in 1841. His residence was originally numbers 29 and 30 Lower Belgrave Place, but he threw them together and renamed them as part of Eccleston Street. He was a self-made man, son of a carpenter. As a boy he used to ride a donkey delivering milk to Sheffield, and was afterwards apprenticed to a wood-carver. Once when he was dining with Samuel Rogers he asked if his host remembered who made a table on which stood a vase which he'd admired. "A common carpenter," said Rogers, surprised, and when he had told how he'd superintended the finishing and placing, Chantrey told him: "I was the carpenter." His best work was done in the Belgrave studio: *The Sleeping Children* monument for Lichfield Cathedral, the bust of Sir Walter Scott, the statue of Watts and the bronze statue of William Pitt for Hanover Square. His statue of Mrs Siddons as the Tragic Muse, for Westminster Abbey, was from the picture by Reynolds. George IV gave him three hundred guineas for a portrait bust. He amassed a fortune of £150,000, and left the Royal Academy £105,000 (with life rent to his widow) in 3 per cent (later 2½ per cent) consols for the purchase of native works of art, the President to receive £300 a year, the Secretary £50.

Sir Thomas More's great house and grounds in Chelsea was bounded on the south by the river-side road and on the west by Beaufort Street. Erasmus described the life of the place.

> "There he converses with his wife, his son, his daughter-in-law, his three daughters and their husbands, with clever grandchildren. There is not any man living so affectionate as he, and he loveth his old wife as well as if she were a young maid . . . though there is none therein but readeth or studieth the liberal sciences, their special care is piety and virtue; there is no quarrelling or intemperate words heard; none seen idle; that worthy gentleman doth not govern with proud and lofty words, but with well-timed and courteous benevolence; everybody performeth his duty, yet is there always alacrity; neither is sober mirth anything wanting."

Indeed, More often joked with and entertained the epigrammatist and playwright John Heywood, who became a sort of superior court jester. He himself was witty and a good actor.

Erasmus speaks too of More's love of animals and interest in their development and dispositions; he kept birds, an ape, a ferret, a weasel, a fox, and many dogs to which he was most tender. He liked, too, to buy foreign curiosities, in which, says Erasmus, "he renews his own pleasure as often as he is witness of the delight of others." The *Percy Anecdotes* tell rather a sad tale of a favourite dog. A maniac vagrant got upstairs while Sir Thomas sat enjoying the view from the top of his gate-house, and tried forcefully to throw him from the battlements, with gay, encouraging cries of "Leap, Tom, leap." Sir Thomas voiced no objection, but said, "Let us first throw this little dog over"; and, that done, "Pretty sport; now go down and bring him up; then we'll try again." The madman obeyed, and the Lord Chancellor, as he then was, made fast the door and called successfully for help.

When a private lawyer, he would take no fees from the poor, from widows or pupils. When he was Chancellor all the causes in the Court of Chancery were cleared up till one day not a suit depended on it, and he had a note made of the date in the records. He refused all gifts from litigants, though common practice was to take bribes from both sides.

Erasmus, who was so touchingly pleased because the English girls thought it civil to kiss the gentlemen, was a brilliant, witty, hypochondriacal and genuinely rather fragile person. He attacked abuses in the church and was not a friend to illiberal insistence on much doctrine, but his endeavour was that reform should come from within the Roman Catholic Church in time to avoid a split, to which he was opposed. Of course, the split came first; much regeneration of the old church after. Erasmus behaved well about Luther, whom he considered a good man but wrong, and was naturally attacked by both sides, since cultivated common sense seldom makes headway when the winds of persecution blow. The successful figures of Reformation and Counter-Reformation, Luther, Calvin and Loyola, were mediaeval people; Erasmus and More belong to the modern world.

The most readable book by Erasmus is his gay, intelligent satire *The Praise of Folly*, dedicated to More, and illustrated by Holbein.

The adjective "Utopian" is often used by people who have never looked into More's *Utopia*. In Utopia all things are owned in common for the common good, though there are bondmen; eggs are hatched in incubators (which existed nowhere else in the world of 1516); a six-hour day is worked alike by men and women—or less should a surplus be produced; the fashion never changes; bride and groom see each other naked before committing themselves to marriage; both are expected to be virgin; martial glory is despised, though men and women too learn to fight in case they must; wars are undertaken only to repel invasion or to deliver an oppressed nation or an ally, and if possible are carried on by mercenaries, though Utopians are brave on demand; the common people of the enemy are pitied; gold is used for chamber-pots that it may not be valued; all religions are tolerated, but ascetic practices are not considered wise, though the practitioner may be holy; atheists, however, are allowed no part in political life; old, widowed women can be priests; (temperate) pleasure is much approved; sufferers from painful and incurable diseases are recommended suicide, but carefully tended if they prefer; cruelty to animals is forbidden; the criminal law is mild (the book opens—so early along this savage branch of our history—with an argument against capital punishment for theft). And life is perhaps somewhat dull, monotonous and lacking in development.

More never had trusted over much to Henry VIII's visits and the royal arm round his neck as they walked. He mounted a peculiarly ricketty scaffold on Tower Hill, remarking, "I pray you, Master Lieutenant, see me safe up; and for my coming down, let me shift for myself."

Afterwards his house became a royal residence. Lucky Ann of Cleves, who accepted Henry VIII's rejection so willingly that he was both shocked and respectful, died at More's mansion in 1557. Poor Catherine Parr, who survived Henry only to marry the yet more odious Admiral Seymour, occupied it with him and the thirteen-year-old Princess Elizabeth, an unfortunate chapter in the girl's life.

Joseph Mallord William Turner, the son of a barber, never had much education or any pretensions to elegance, a bluff, red-faced man who made hearty jokes and was fond of his friends, but had a good deal of reserve. About 1847 or 1848 he closed his Queen Anne Street house, disappeared from his usual haunts, and when he visited a friend or met one in a gallery would not tell his address. Only when he was dying was he tracked to 119 Cheyne Walk, where he was living with a Mrs Booth, whose name he had adopted and whom he had known long before in her Margate boarding house. He painted several pictures there, though his greatest work was done. They would often go together to the waterside, and Greaves the boatman would row them over to Battersea. Turner called her 'old 'un' and she called him 'dear,' and nursed him when he fell ill in 1851. When Doctor Price was sent for from Margate and told him there was no hope of recovery, Turner said, "Take a glass of sherry, and look at me again." The doctor took the glass of sherry, but could not change his opinion. And shortly after Turner died.

Whistler lived, at one time and another, at four houses in Cheyne Row, numbers 101, 96, 21 and 74. Between 96 and 21 he spent a year in Italy, took various London lodgings, lived at 13 Tite Street, 454 Fulham Road, and in the Vale, Chelsea. He was a fine Chelsea figure, who dressed fantastically and would sometimes pay calls with pink bows on his shoes. His eyes were bright under bushy eyebrows and a white lock stood up among his raven curls. He moved to 96 Cheyne Row in 1867. A man named Barthe, to whom he owed money for tapestries, called there one evening for payment, pushed his way in, found Whistler painting by candlelight, with sons of Greaves the boatman holding candles. "And Vistlaire he say, 'You ze very man I vant; hold a candle!' And I hold a candle. And Vistlaire he paint, and he paint, and zen he take ze picture, and he go downstairs, and he get in ze cab, and he drive off, and we hold ze candle, and I see him no more. Mon dieu, il est terrible, ce Vistlaire!" He was still at 96 in 1873 when he painted Carlyle, whose comment on Watts's portrait of him had been that he'd like Watts to know it was his habit to wear clean linen. Carlyle thought Whistler the most absurd creature on the face of the earth.

At 93 Cheyne Walk was born Mrs Gaskell (1810–1865), that admirable writer whose novels, never without tenderness, are sometimes so strong and absolutely uncompromising.

D. G. Rossetti moved to 15 Cheyne Walk in 1862 after his wife's death, and kept it till his own death twenty years later. For a time Swinburne lived there with him. There was thought of Meredith sharing too, for it is a roomy house, but he was off in a flash. There is a story of a schoolroom sort of squabble between him and Rossetti; another theory is that Rossetti looked too revolting at breakfast eating rows of poached eggs.

Fanny Cornforth (then Mrs Hughes) was installed nearby at 36 Royal Avenue; her constant presence as Rossetti's hostess was vexing to some of the guests. There was plenty of company and plenty of fun in the sixties (Whistler was one of the household friends), and in spite of memories of Lizzie Siddal and the despair to come, a happy life was led for a while at Number 16, imagination's perfect pattern for Chelsea.

The house was overful of picturesque objects; the outside was never refurbished; the garden, forlorn with weeds instead of flowers, was full of fantastic birds and animals, whom Rossetti understood and liked. He bought a Brahmin bull whose eyes made him think of Jane Morris. He wanted a lion, but the heating was too difficult. He wanted an elephant. When Browning asked why, he said he'd teach it to clean the windows, so that people would ask whose house it was and his pictures would be advertised. He said a lot of pleasant silly things. Years later he said, on mislaying his hat, "Sunk into the earth, by God."

And now Mr Charles Augustus Howell came into the life of Rossetti and Swinburne. He was half Portuguese, a buccaneering type, a clever agent, a lively raconteur and a liar. He came to London (not his first visit) in 1864 and was Ruskin's secretary for a while. Asked why he employed such a man, Ruskin said he would neither give Howell a character nor let his wife and family starve. Ruskin and Rossetti were both fascinated by him; so to some extent was Whistler (who in due course inherited him) and Swinburne, "the demoniac youth," as Ruskin called him. Later Swinburne was to report evil of "the polecat Howell"; there'd been trouble over silly improper letters, such as Swinburne too often wrote, which had fallen into the wrong hands. It was Howell, not a discreet man, who was entrusted with resurrecting Rossetti's sonnets from Lizzie's buried red hair. He would have been an excellent agent had he not embezzled and stolen. Theodore Watts-Dunton swept down to rescue his beloved Swinburne (who spent his last thirty years with him at the Pines, Putney Hill) and disentangled Rossetti's dealings with Howell at the same time. Rossetti rather liked Howell, as he much liked Fanny, through all the darker years of suspicion, persecution mania, whisky, chloral, illness and quarrels; perhaps there was nothing much left of which to suspect them. Howell visited Rossetti at Birchington just before his death, much to Hall Caine's disgust, and made him laugh; he said he had written most of Ruskin's books and was now buying horses for the King of Portugal. A strange fate was waiting for Howell. In 1890 he was found in a Chelsea gutter, outside a public-house, with his throat cut and a ten-shilling piece clenched between his teeth. At once objects of art lost by Swinburne, Rossetti and Whistler began to reappear. "He was really wonderful," said Whistler.

George Eliot (Mary Ann Evans, 1819–1880) went to 4 Cheyne Walk after her marriage to J. W. Cross, lived there for three weeks and then died of a chill caught at a concert. After the liaison of twenty-four years or so with G. H. Lewes, who died in 1878, married life was very brief; from March till late December.

She was justly celebrated in her own day. *Adam Bede* was immediately so successful that a Mr Liggins claimed to be the author; and there were finer, more fascinating books to come. She was a woman to command respect, the recognition of personal nobility; but her living in open sin was not altogether an assimilable thing. If she rather solemnly welcomed incense-burning at her literary shrine, it may have been for lack of the odour of sanctity. For example, Professor T. H. Huxley would visit her and Lewes in their St John's Wood house from his, but he would never take his wife; he was an iconoclast, but not indiscriminately; he was also a puritan. She wrote an inscription for Lewes on the manuscript of *The Mill on the Floss*, beginning "To my beloved husband." Apart from Mr Cross's kindness and companionability, one wonders, outside 4 Cheyne Walk, whether she felt special satisfaction just in being married.

In 1834 Leigh Hunt was living at 10 (it was 4 then) Upper Cheyne Row, when he suggested that 24 (at that time 5) Cheyne Row would suit Carlyle. Carlyle took it, and remained till his death in early 1881. His wife, a remarkable woman, died fifteen years before he did, leaving him to become more joyless and morose; and to grieve that their marriage, a genuine tie, not without elements to respect, had proved so unsatisfactory. At this house, now a museum, Carlyle wrote all his books, except *Sartor Resartus*, and some of the essays; and here came many of the most distinguished Londoners and London visitors of his day whether he wanted them or not. Leigh and Marianne Hunt remained his neighbours in Chelsea for seven years of anxious poverty, he working away very hard in the floating printed nightdress he wore for writing, she a tiresome, untidy woman always borrowing spoons and saucepans from Jane Carlyle and forgetting to give them back. Oddly, Carlyle and Hunt appreciated each other with warmth and justice, and one of the sunny memories of tempestuous 24 Cheyne Row is Hunt's arrival with some news so pleasant that Mrs Carlyle gaily kissed him. And back at 10 Upper Cheyne Row he wrote what is the best remembered of his poems except *Abou Ben Adhem*:

> Jenny kissed me when we met,
> Jumping from the chair she sat in . . .

Oscar Wilde as well as Whistler had a house in Tite Street. His was number 16. Here he had an interview with his dedicated enemy, Queensberry, in which he bore himself well. (Surely there is poetic justice in the harsh fact that Queensberry died with persecution mania, believing that he was being harried to the tomb by what he called "the Oscar Wilders.") Here Wilde received the blackmailing visit of a cheap skate named Allen, who had the "prose-poem" to Lord Alfred Douglas which included the words, "It is a marvel that those rose-red lips of yours should have been made no less for music of song than for madness of kisses." "Open to misinterpretation," commented Sir Beerbohm Tree to Wilde, handing over a copy which had been sent him. The following dialogue opens with the same thought from Allen:

"A very curious construction can be put on that letter."

"Art is rarely intelligible to the criminal classes."

"A man has offered me £60 for it."

"If you will take my advice, you will go to that man and sell my letter to him for £60. I myself have never received so large a sum for any prose work of that length, but I am glad to find there is someone in England who considers a letter of mine worth £60."

"Er—the man is out of town."

"He is sure to come back."

But on finding Allen was hard up, Wilde gave him ten shillings, and another half sovereign to his associate Clibborn, who suddenly brought him the prose poem as a present because he had been both cool and kind.

"I am afraid you are leading a wonderfully wicked life," said Wilde.

"There is good and bad in all of us," said Clibborn.

"You are a born philosopher," said Wilde.

(Oscar Wilde was never proved to have corrupted any youthful innocence whatever, and his good-humour was beyond praise. The most damning evidence against him was all found by a voluntary agent, an actor in one of his plays inexplicably bent on hounding him. This was told to Wilde after he had served his sentence. All he said of such groundless, ruinous malice was an indulgent, "How absurd of Brookfield!")

And into 16 Tite Street Wilde's creditors put bailiffs; for his plays were taken off, no one dared buy his books, and Mme Sarah Bernhardt ignored the request to advance something on royalties for her agreed production of *Salome*. Wilde was sold up, and the sale was conducted scandalously; valuable pictures and first editions went for all but nothing, and many interesting possessions were quite simply stolen.

The Earl of Surrey, one of the two first English sonnet-writers, in the reign of Henry VIII, lived in Norfolk Street, Lambeth, on the south side of the river.

It was when William Blake was living at 23 Hercules Road, Lambeth (where he wrote and painted much), that a caller found him and his wife Catherine naked in the garden, reciting, in character, Adam and Eve passages from *Paradise Lost*.

The tuneful Arthur Sullivan was born in Lambeth in Bolwell Street, and lived in Victoria Street later.

The associations with Westminster Abbey are so overwhelming that only a few of the lesser known kind can be touched on. Who is the only female novelist buried in the "National Valhalla"? No one will grudge it, for it is the first of the tribe: Mrs Aphra Behn, licentious in life and in pen, also a playwright and a beautiful spy, of the reign of Charles II.

And who would suppose that Adam Lindsay Gordon could have

Oscar Wilde

found his way to burial there? He was born in 1833 in the Azores; he was educated in England; he went young, he was only twenty, to shift for himself alone in Australia. He cut a dashing figure enough, one of the Australian Mounted Police, member for Victoria in the House of Assembly, horse-breaker and livery-stable keeper, the best gentleman steeple-chase-rider on the continent. A fall, financial loss, fear that he might not be recognized or remembered as a poet; and he blew out his brains near Melbourne in June of 1870.

> The yarns Jack Hall invented, and
> the songs Jem Roper sang;
> But where are now Jem Roper and Jack Hall?

Surely *The Sick Stock-rider* is remembered; certainly one verse of A. L. Gordon's is better known than is the author's name.

> Life is mostly froth and bubble;
> Two things stand like stone—
> Kindness in another's trouble,
> Courage in your own.

One tends to make a slip of the tongue and find one has said "courage in another's trouble"; even that is not so easy.

And again, many know the lines:

> I do not love thee, Dr Fell,
> The reason why I cannot tell;
> But this I know, and know full well,
> I do not love thee, Dr Fell.

who do not know that they were written by Tom Brown (1663–1704) to a Dean of Christ's College, Oxford; and that this Tom Brown, "of facetious memory," said Addison, though shifty and disreputable, wrote a nice book on London called *Amusements, Serious and Comic*, and sleeps long in the cloisters of Westminster Abbey.

Edmund Spenser died of a broken heart in King Street, Westminster —it ran parallel to Whitehall—in 1599. He was exhausted, and Ben Jonson says that there was "lack of bread," and that he refused twenty pieces from the Earl of Essex because he had no time to spend them.

Chaucer leased a house in Westminster in 1399, when, after financial troubles and his greatest literary achievement, he received a pension again, from Henry IV. He died on 25th October 1400. His house adjoined the White Rose Tavern and abutted on the old Lady Chapel of the Abbey; it was demolished in 1502 to make room for the gorgeous mausoleum of Henry VII.

Mrs Bracegirdle: "The Indian Queen"

Edmund Kean: "The Theatrical Atlas"

Nell Gwyn

"The Beggar's Opera": from a Print by Bartolozzi

From Scotland Yard, S.W.1, in 1863 Messrs. Walker & Whicker were sent to Warsaw at the request of Grand Duke Constantine to confer with and advise the Russian authorities on the subject of police organization. It was Mr Whicker who, in 1860, was much blamed for the cruel absurdity of believing that Constance Kent, so innocent seeming and so young, could be guilty of a hideous crime. He was heard muttering, "Well, nothing more of this murder will be known till Constance Kent confesses"; and, if it was a laugh, he laughed last.

The Colonial Office in Whitehall was once Melbourne House. The Melbournes had earlier lived in Piccadilly where is now the block of flats called Albany, and had exchanged with the Duke of York and Albany for the Whitehall mansion. Here was passed the early married life of that charming, clever, tolerant William Lamb, who lived to be the young Queen Victoria's Lord Melbourne, and his wild wife Lady Caroline, daughter of Sheridan's Lady Bessborough and niece of the most famous of all Duchesses of Devonshire.

Whatever one may think of the reckless exhibitionist Lady Caroline Lamb, it was rough on her that the hard, worldly mother-in-law who hated her should be Byron's great friend and confidante.

At Melbourne House (the Colonial Office) Byron called, after his first meeting with Caroline Lamb at Holland House, and gave her a rose. And Caroline, who not only respected but devotedly and for ever loved her husband, fell in love too for ever with a handsome poet. From Melbourne House in 1812 Caroline ran away—harassed by her cold, angry mother-in-law; by her charming, anxious mother, Lady Bessborough; by her own feelings; by all but her husband, so gently, kindly cynical, so affectionately, ruefully enchanted and amused with her follies. And Byron himself brought her back, having sought and found her at the entreaty of both the older ladies. In 1816 the Lamb family persuaded William that her mad scandals brought too much ridicule on them all, wrecked his career and warped his parents' lives; they won his consent to a legal separation. They met in conclave; the lawyers came; and Caroline waited upstairs submissively ready to sign any document that William told her to, for she wanted to be just. He went upstairs to ask her a question. They waited for his return. Time passed. She must be making a horrible scene. They had better rescue him and appease the waiting lawyers. And upstairs they found William in a large armchair, and Caroline on his lap feeding him with thin bread and butter.

The lawyers went away.

Years later, after Byron's death in 1824, after the delayed separation at long last in 1825 and all the subsequent cherishing visits he paid her, after she had died adrift and tamed and bewildered in 1828, after the *Literary Gazette* had written of her love for her friends, her tolerance of enemies, her sweetness to the poor, adding crisply "the world does not want good hearts but regulated minds . . ." when he was old, and despite Mrs Norton's gentleness, William told a friend that Caro was the only woman he had ever really loved.

In 1861 Hungerford Market stood where Charing Cross Station now is, Northumberland Street ran directly to the river, and the river itself —where now the railway crosses it—was spanned by the Hungerford suspension bridge. On 12th July a Major William Murray landed at Hungerford bridge by steamboat and was accosted by a total stranger, who, however, gave himself a plausible status through a business pretext which bore on genuine interests of Murray's. The stranger led Murray to his chambers nearby on the first floor of 16 Northumberland Street. Here he shot him, first in the back of the neck and, five minutes later on perceiving signs of life, in the right temple. No one in the building took the least notice of the shots, for the occupant of those particular chambers, a money-lending solicitor named Roberts, had prepared for the murder of Major Murray by taking up target practice at least a month earlier. But in spite of this practice, Murray was still alive, and shortly after he appeared streaming with blood and shouting for help at the window, having battered his assailant into an appalling condition with the tongs and a bottle. Roberts's chambers were encrusted with dust and dirt, but splendidly furnished in Louis Philippe style, with gilt and looking-glasses and boule and ormolu; now the place was coated with blood, the wreckage indescribable. The wounded Major Murray jumped twenty feet down into a small yard between iron railings. Roberts could not move. Both men were taken to Charing Cross Hospital, and Roberts' death-bed story was that Murray had come about a loan, had shot himself in the neck and then demoniacally attacked the money-lender. The ex-Major was still bewildered by the whole affair.

Murray was keeping a very pretty girl named Anne Maria Moody, whom he allowed to use his name and by whom he had a child. Some three or four years before the Northumberland Street blood-bath she was short of money. She did not want to trouble her protector, whom she felt to be as generous as he could afford. She borrowed £15 from Roberts, to whom she had been recommended; from that moment his pursuit of her never ceased. She could not catch up with the loan and repay; she kept consenting to see him clandestinely to keep him quiet. And Roberts, the prosperous solicitor and bill-discounter, husband, father of a grown-up son, centre of a family circle, became so obsessed with the violence of his dark passion that he tried to commit murder and was himself destroyed amid the dust, the empty bottles and the fine ormolu furniture.

"Justifiable homicide," said the jury, reasonably. Major William Murray died at the age of eighty-eight in 1907.

VII

The West End; Strand, Covent Garden, Soho, Haymarket, etcetera

The few steps from Fleet Street to the Strand take one from the City to "the West End"; business lies behind one, and pleasure could easily begin either at Drury Lane Theatre, not far northward, or at the Savoy Hotel, but a little way along on the south side of the street.

Off the south side of the Strand, before the Savoy is reached coming from the east, run Arundel Street, Norfolk Street, and Surrey Street, with Howard Street crossing the second on its way from the first to the third.

In Howard Street at the house of a Mrs Dorothy Brown lodged Anne Bracegirdle (*c.* 1663–1748), the celebrated actress, known by the custom of her time as Mrs Bracegirdle, but not married. Indeed, though her portrayal of love on the stage was most disturbing to the gentlemen of the audience, she was generally accounted both ignorant of that passion and impregnably chaste.

There were some rumours about her and Mr Congreve. He lived round the corner in Surrey Street, and they were very close friends for a long while; though when he was nearing sixty, partly blind with cataracts and lamed by the gout, he was swept off by the young Duchess of Marlborough and remained engrossed with her, and indeed she with him, till his death in 1729. Leigh Hunt thought he ought to have left his £10,000 to Mrs Bracegirdle. Johnson said it should have gone to his Congreve relations who needed it. He did leave the beautiful Anne £200, though the bulk went to his Duchess already overwhelmingly wealthy. She showed her appreciation, however. She buried him with great pomp; she spent most of the legacy on a splendid diamond necklace worn in his honour; and is said to have had a clock-work ivory statue of him to keep her company at table and a wax doll in his image whose feet her doctors had regularly to treat for gout.

Despite the Congreve gossip, Mrs Bracegirdle's chastity was so widely and solidly credited that the Earl of Halifax and the Dukes of Devonshire and Dorset, with some others, made up a purse of £800 as a testimonial to it, which they brought, swords in hand, from a coffee-house to Howard Street.

Captain Richard Hill conceived for her a passion that separated him from all content and came between him and the sun. After she had rejected his hand offered in marriage, he consulted with his friend the profligate Lord Mohun, and on the night of 9th December 1692, having found out her evening's plans, they stationed a coach in Drury Lane by the Horseshoe Tavern and hired six soldiers to force her into it. At about ten o'clock, with her mother, her brother and a Mr Page, she came from supping in Prince's Street and turned down Drury Lane. A soldier seized her in his arms, and on Mr Page's seeking to free her, Captain Hill struck at his head with his sword, though the blow only wounded his hand. Meanwhile the lady's screams roused the local rabble in her defence, whereat Lord Mohun, seeing the attempt had failed, insisted that he and his friend would see her home. Brave Mr Page came too, and entered Mrs Dorothy Brown's house with her for her better protection.

From Drury Lane across the Strand to Howard Street, Captain Richard Hill had not ceased ranting on the subject of revenge. He saw his rejection in terms of a rival, and picked on Will Mountfort, the finest actor in Betterton's company after the great man himself. Mr Mountfort's wife was an attractive woman and a most brilliant, versatile comedienne. Apparently they were happily married and Mrs Bracegirdle was on good terms with both. However, like Mrs Bracegirdle herself, he was a magnificent stage lover, and to see the two playing opposite each other must have been dreadful to Captain Hill. Moreover, Mountfort was a very handsome man.

When she was safely in her home Mrs Bracegirdle sent Ann Jones, the maidservant, running to the Norfolk Street house to ask if Mr Mountfort were within. Ann Jones must have been flustered and excited, for on hearing he was out she ran off and had to be sent again with a message to his wife, begging that he should be sought for and warned that Lord Mohun and Captain Hill, with no good intention, waited for him in the street. He was sought for in vain, while Lord Mohun encouraged his friend by sending to the Horseshoe Tavern for canary.

When Will Mountfort strolled into Howard Street, the landlady, Mrs Brown, called to him to keep away. He scorned to do so. Lord

Mohun embraced him warmly, on which he said, "I wonder, my lord, that you would justify the rudeness of Captain Hill or keep company with such a pitiful fellow." Captain Hill said that he would justify himself, and to do this he mortally wounded his fellow man and fled like a thief in the night. Lord Mohun was taken by the Duchy Watch, with his sword still in its sheath.

Lord Mohun was tried and acquitted as an accomplice in the murder. He, the captain's manservant, and Ann Jones, the maid, all testified that both the men had fought. But Mountfort on his death-bed swore to Mr Page that he was run through the body before he had time to draw his sword.

A month later Mrs Bracegirdle and Mrs Mountfort triumphed in Congreve's first comedy, with the great and good Betterton. There was also Mr Verbruggen, a powerful actor of a rougher type than Mountfort, who married the widowed Susanna Mountfort that same year. Alas, for the Verbruggens; her mind became deranged. She was perfectly gentle, and allowed to roam freely in her house. One night she escaped and went to the back stage of Drury Lane Theatre. They were playing *Hamlet*. She pushed aside the Ophelia, for she knew the part, and gave as her last performance a poignant rendering of the mad girl.

Lord Mohun's end was suitable. He and the fourth Duke of Hamilton killed each other in Hyde Park by the Achilles statue. Lady Mohun, seeing her husband's corpse laid on the best bed, was only concerned that his blood stained the costly covers and scolded without mercy the men who brought him.

Macklin Street, off Drury Lane, was once called Lewknor Street, and there Nell Gwyn is first heard of, running errands for Mother Ross's brothel and singing bawdy songs at taverns. She was a hungry child of thirteen, and had a lover, Richard, a link-boy, who bought her stockings to cover her chilblains. She may have sold oranges for Orange Moll, who had the concession at Drury Lane Theatre. She made her début at the age of fifteen in 1665 in Dryden's play about Montezuma, and the famous actor Hart became her tutor and her lover. Pepys assures us that she was no good in tragedy, but an irresistible comedienne, and she had such a happy gift with prologues and epilogues that Dryden wrote them specially for her to rattle off. She had an unsuccessful love affair with Lord Buckhurst before she caught the King's eye. Even when she did, he preferred for a while the dancer Moll Davies, to whom Nell once gave sweets filled with a strong purgative before a night appointment with the King. In 1670 she finally won Charles, tearing gaily through the Prologue of Dryden's *Almanzor and Almahide or the Conquest of Granada by the Spaniards* in boy's clothes and a hat larger than a cartwheel. He took her away for good and all, and she loved him ever after. Everyone forgives her her sins, because she loved much, and because she was fearless and funny. She deeply loved Charles, her sister and her mother, and was good to the poor. It was typical that when the crowd threw dirt and stones at her coach by mistake for the Duchess of Portsmouth's, she stuck out her charming head and bellowed cheerfully, "No, no, good people; it is the Protestant whore!"

She is popular too because hers is a Cinderella story, not like that of poor "Perdita" Robinson, who in 1779 also won a royal lover from Drury Lane stage, was true and good to her prince, only to be discarded and cut face to face in the Park. He gave her no money; her father had spent his fortune and hers on trying to civilize the Eskimos; and being as notorious as the sun at noonday, she was not allowed even to return to the theatre. Charles James Fox got her a pension of £300 from the tax-payers' pockets; and she had a little basket of flowers painted on her carriage panels because she so longed for a coat-of-arms and that was the best she could do about it.

Bow Street, running south from Long Acre about midway between Drury Lane and Covent Garden, but not all the way to the Strand, is associated with many famous names, as the tablet on the Midland Bank tells us.

Henry Fielding (1707–1754) lived there when he was made Justice of the Peace for Westminster in December 1748; he had already written *Joseph Andrews or the Virtuous Footman* and *Tom Jones*, and was very active as a magistrate. He was handsome and merry, affectionate and hard working, a devoted husband and excellent company. He had endless worries with money and ill-health and great sorrow for the death of his wife, but he had much positive happiness, and his second wife was good to him.

Wycherley, the Restoration dramatist, chose wives with less discrimination. He was unfortunate in his first marriage, scandalous in his second. As a handsome young rake his pursuit was of pleasure rather than happiness; and indeed the first is more easily caught and, so long as one will be pleased, the best known substitute for the second. His old age was vexed and vexing. Macaulay is very censorious about him, and inaccurate too; no less than Congreve, he was a

William Wycherley

well-liked man and evoked real warmth in friendship. Besides, *The Gentleman Dancing-Master* and *The Country Wife* are funnier than Macaulay owns.

Wycherley's first play was produced during Lent in 1671, some few months after Barbara Palmer's rise from Countess of Castlemaine to Duchess of Cleveland. Her coach passing his in Pall Mall, she thrust herself halfway through the window and saluted him with roars of laughter as the son of a whore. This he recognized as an allusion to a song in the play, which ended:

> Great Wits and great Braves
> Have always a Punk to their Mother.

He had his coach turned, overtook hers, and made an appointment.

Charles II was friendly about the liaison. It was Buckingham who at first was jealous, though his wrath swiftly changed to affection. Soon after, Wycherley was sick at his lodgings in Bow Street and the King visited him, sat by his bed, and gave him money to try what a change of air could do for him.

Wycherley's last comedy was successfully performed not later than the spring of 1674, when he was about thirty-four years of age. And now, with forty-one years and some odd months of life left to him, the tide of his fortunes turned to a long, slow ebb. Charles II chose him as an accomplished man to conduct the education of his natural son the young Duke of Richmond, and Wycherley in high feather went junketting off to Tonbridge. In a book-shop he found a handsome woman buying his play *The Plain Dealer*; she was the rich widow, Lady Drogheda. He married her in 1679 without telling the king, and worse, tried unsuccessfully to keep it secret. Charles may also have known of his courageous (though bad) verses on his old friend Buckingham's fall from favour and imprisonment in the Tower:

> Your late Disgrace is but the Court's Disgrace,
> As its false accusation but your Praise, etc.

Wycherley was now out of court favour, and his wife was no consolation; terrible scenes took place in Bow Street. He could not even meet his friends at the Cock Tavern opposite his house but, for fear of her brawling, he had to leave the windows open, while she sat watching, watching across the street, lest at any time a woman should join the company.

Her death in 1681 and the legacy of her fortune only led to lawsuits and imprisonment for debt, till James II, seeing a good performance of *The Plain Dealer*, pitied a man he must have remembered as gay and handsome, paid his debts, and gave him a pension of £200 a year. He came soon after into his father's property, strictly tied up on an heir-at-law with whom he jangled, and his expensive tastes kept him always financially embarrassed. He wrote poems which were not even good verse; *Miscellany Poems*, published 1704, were on the whole beneath criticism. His memory was strangely impaired from a fever for decades before his death. He would sometimes repeat the same thought within ten lines of a poem he was composing and be amazed and obliged when this was pointed out to him. He would read someone's book at night and passages of it would come back to him as his own new inspiration in the morning. He mourned the decline of his personal beauty, and sighed when he looked on Lely's portrait of him at twenty-eight.

He was sixty-four when he met a boy of sixteen named Alexander Pope, recognized his genius, took him under his wing, and showed him the vices of the town. Pope was enchanted with the old lion, whose plays were still famous, and soon found himself at the strange employment of revising and polishing poems not worth his attention. Their friendship was real and lasted till Wycherley died, aged seventy-five, but there were estrangements. In these Wycherley's trustless memory may have played a part, as well as the hopelessness of Pope's task. He was cutting blocks with a razor. It was not possible both to slash adequately and spare the old man's feelings. The verses were not only bad, they were ribald and indecent after the fashion of their writer's youth; taste had changed and the rising stars wrote with more propriety.

Eleven days before his death Wycherley married a young girl, who thus became entitled to a jointure of £400 a year from the estate entailed upon his "damned nephew," who had refused to let him settle his debts by selling any part of it. He paid the debts with some money the lady brought him, obliged her by providing her with an income, and plagued his enemy. It was a situation fit for one of his plays, for, though he did not know it, she was the cast-off mistress of the man who recommended her merits to his protection. He asked her but one favour; "My dear, . . . never marry an old man again." Pope found him more patient on his death-bed than in health, and not much afraid to die.

At 6 Bow Street, Charles Macklin, Peg Woffington and David

Garrick set up as a threesome. Other men had a share in her favours too, and once Garrick had to leave her bed in a hurry for a noble arriving at the front door. He left his wig behind, and Peg explained it away as make-up for a "breeches part"; for as soon as actresses were allowed on the stage they made up for those lost Elizabethan years by starring in the men's parts as well as their own, and she was never more popular than as Sir Harry Wildair. "I've played this part so many times that half the town thinks I'm a man," she said to Quin. "And the other half *knows* that you are not," he responded. Garrick meant to marry her, but besides being unfaithful, she was extravagant, temperamental and tempestuous; they quarrelled. His marriage in 1749 to Violetta, the beautiful Viennese dancer, was exceptionally happy; they were devoted to each other and were never one night apart. But he did not forget that he had once loved Peg Woffington, and was very good to her at the end of her life in spite of her bad temper.

The violent and formidable Macklin was a pioneer of the new, natural style of acting, which Garrick developed to such perfection alike in tragedy, comedy and farce. Macklin broke a long-standing tradition when he played his grim, tragic Shylock, which rocked the theatre with applause and quite terrified George II; for before that Shylock had degenerated into a comic character. Doggett, a most capable comedian who founded a prize rowing competition for Thames waterman, had been much appreciated in the rôle. Pope said of Macklin's triumph,

This is the Jew
That Shakespeare drew,

and King George, asked by Robert Walpole to suggest a way of frightening the House of Commons, said, "What do you think of sending them to see that Irishman play Shylock?"

It was Macklin's habit at night to wash all over with brandy and then sleep in his clothes.

It is impossible to read Colley Cibber and not believe that Betterton, Mountfort, etc., were wonderful actors. But the tragic style was formal, declamatory and slow. Garrick's speed and life-like manner were a revolution. He studied life, and even visited Bedlam before playing Lear. The new style lost nothing in intensity. Once when Garrick said to the First Murderer in Macbeth, "There's blood upon thy face," he so horrified him that the man put up his hand to feel for it, exclaiming in consternation, "Is there, by God!"

Garrick had a happy life. Though he had the (then) usual share of extraordinary rows and riots in audiences, he was one of the most successful actors who ever lived. His marriage was made in heaven and did it credit. He had delightful friends. And he took care of his money.

Covent Garden Theatre in early days was in tremendous rivalry with Drury Lane. At times the performances of great stars on the two stages assumed the quality of duels; duels at a distance, like a chess fight by post—Garrick *v.* Quin, Kean *v.* Kemble, and so on. But my particular Covent Garden ghost is Ruskin in a temper with the pantomime because the Forty Thieves were nothing but a lot of girls, and because the audience hugely applauded them just for lighting forty cigars, after making no response to a charming, joyous dance performed by a little girl of eight or nine and two men dressed as a donkey.

At 20 Russell Street, Covent Garden, Charles Lamb wrote the *Essays of Elia*.

In Maiden Lane J. M. W. Turner was born, at No. 26, since demolished. In this street too lived Andrew Marvell, an honest man, a witty man of pre-Restoration taste, a man who continued to praise Cromwell while giving Charles II a fair chance to win his regard, and a most excellent poet. Voltaire lodged here for about three years, 1726–1729. Bolingbroke introduced him to Pope and his circle; he met Chesterfield and the Herveys and the Duchess of Marlborough; he made friends with Gay; he called on Congreve, who chose to play the man of quality and fashion rather than the wit, and Voltaire said, "If he had been only a gentleman I should not have come thither to visit him."

Just north in Henrietta Street Jane Austen stayed with her brother and, a few steps north again, Coleridge once lived at 10 King Street.

Coleridge lived too at 21 Buckingham Street, off the other (south) side of the Strand. Pepys lived at No. 12 from 1684 till 1688, and then moved till 1701 to No. 14—a house which includes, among other distinguished patrons, the artist William Etty (1787–1849), Robert Marley, Earl of Oxford (1661–1724) and our old friend Clarkson Stanfield.

Rudyard Kipling (1865–1936) lived at 43 Villiers Street from September 1890 till he had a breakdown of health in the following year. He lodged in three small, unkempt rooms over the useful establishment of Sausage-King Harris, who would blow one out for 2*d*. Opposite was Gatti's Music Hall, where the atmosphere set for him the pattern of his first *Barrack-Room Ballads*, while "an elderly but upright" barmaid whom he took there suggested, with the story of a friend, his *Mary pity Women*. *The Light that Failed* was written in Villiers Street. A plaque upon his first and last London residence commemorates a light that flamed.

Heinrich Heine spent three months at 32 Craven Street in 1827, and was not happy. He admired London, but felt it oppressive. And there was snow in April.

From the top of the steeple of St Martin's-in-the-Fields, Trafalgar Square, on 1st June 1727, Volante or Violanti (the wire-walker who befriended the ragged Irish waif Peg Woffington and gave her her chance on the stage) descended head foremost by a rope, with arms and legs extended, over the houses in St Martin's Lane, a distance of about three hundred yards in half a minute.

Mrs Centlivre (*c.* 1667–1723) lived near St Martin's-in-the-Fields with her third husband, Joseph Centlivre, who was head cook to Queen Anne with the disconcerting title of "Yeoman of the Mouth." She had been a popular provincial actress and a highly successful dramatist; a hundred and ten years after her death Leigh Hunt recorded that her plays were acted as often as if they were new. A great beauty, a good linguist, witty and good-natured, she was accorded a line in Pope's disobliging *Dunciad* for having written in her childhood a ballad unfriendly to his translation of Homer.

North of Trafalgar Square and Leicester Square, extending westward, Soho, between Charing Cross Road, Oxford Street and Regent Street, has sheltered many illustrious people in various stages of prosperity or lack of it. One of the least prosperous was Thomas de Quincey when, having run away from school and wandered for a while in Wales, he arrived in 1802 at the age of seventeen. He had already had a breakdown in health and for two months he was houseless, sleeping around in doorways. He walked about at night with a gentle prostitute named Ann, of less than sixteen years. He must, one feels, have been rather in the way and not very helpful to trade. She was a dear girl, unsurpassed by the whole tribe of golden-hearted prostitutes in fiction. It was on the steps of a house in Soho Square, where they sat resting, that De Quincey so collapsed with illness that she ran and bought him port wine and spices in Oxford Street, though she herself could scarcely afford to live. He believed that this restoring comfort saved his life.

He had obtained a lodging, a queer one indeed, at 61 (then 38) Greek

Street, before he lost Ann. It happened that an acquaintance lent him £10. He gave her some of it, and went briefly to Windsor to seek help from a family friend, arranging that three nights later, and if necessary each succeeding night, she should wait for him in Soho at the corner of Titchfield Street. Again and again he stood at the appointed place. He asked and sought for her throughout the district. He never found a clue to what had happened to her. It could even have been something good.

Number 61 Greek Street belonged to Mr Brunell-Brown, a rascally attorney who had his office there, but slept each night in a different part of London to dodge creditors and bailiffs. This rogue loved literature. After a few weeks his young lodger could no longer pay, and the lawyer was kind and let him sleep in one of the cheerless empty rooms and eat the scraps, if any, from his breakfast table. There was already a forlorn, mysterious waif in the cheerless house where rats scampered at night; a little girl drudge, hungry, scared, not above ten years old, not interesting or pleasing. De Quincey slept on the floor with this poor child in his arms, to keep her warm and protect her from the ghosts she feared. He left her to the ghosts when, reconciled to his guardians, he was sent from Soho to Oxford. At Oxford he took to opium as a pain-killer, and later leaped to fame with his *Confessions of an English Opium-eater*. Later too he tried to find the little girl, but as vainly as he had sought for Ann.

Mary Elizabeth Braddon (1837–1915) was born in Soho Square. Of some seventy-five novels the best known is the one which made her name in 1862, *Lady Audley's Secret*, the tale of a spirited little golden-haired murderess. It reached its eighth three-volume edition within three months. She married when she was thirty-seven the publisher Mr John Maxwell, and continued to be most successful in her career. Tennyson, for example, found her books enthralling. She liked to illustrate the high spots of her stories in advance, not for publication but as a synopsis to work on. Frith spoke warmly of her drawing of Lady Audley pushing her first husband down a well, and wondered why he never took her advice on subjects for his own pictures.

In Soho Square, too, was the gilded vice house of Mrs Cornelys, who later fared so unluckily in Knightsbridge.

In Greek Street was born Douglas Jerrold, best known for *Mrs Caudle's Curtain Lectures*, published in book form in 1846 after appearing in *Punch*.

Mozart lodged in Frith Street in 1763, an exquisite infant prodigy turned seven years old, on a professional tour of Europe begun when he was six.

Hazlitt died at 6 Frith Street, 18th September 1830, after the final comment, "Well, I've had a happy life." It was scarcely true. His marriages were unsuccessful. His love affair was humiliating and frantic. His literary success was less than he deserved. He had many disappointments. Pain, ill-health and money troubles shadowed his last years. Nevertheless, he led the sort of life that he chose, mixed with the people he liked, never put himself out for public opinion, politeness or prudence. His summing up cannot be disregarded.

Shelley, expelled from Oxford for atheism, took rooms at 15 Poland Street with his friend Thomas Jefferson Hogg. Hogg had found him more than difficult to please in the search for lodgings, but he was finally won by the Poland Street wallpaper, luscious with vine-leaves and grapes. "We must stay here for ever," whispered Shelley. He left within a year for his hurriedly arranged elopement with Harriett Westbrook, who found nothing for it three years later but to drown herself in the Serpentine.

Colonel Francis Charteris, the too-successful card-player and avaricious libertine, lived with his poor wife in Poland Street. He frequented a bordello in Golden Square and may have shown restraint in his wife's home. It was certainly very different from the notorious house of his grass-widowerhood in George Street, Hanover Square.

In 28 Poland Street, William Blake wrote *Songs of Innocence*. There the spirit of his dead brother Robert advised him on engraving; after Robert's death he had seen his soul ascend through the ceiling clapping hands for joy. His wife, the invaluable and devoted Catherine, uneducated daughter of a market gardener, helped him with his work and always cherished him.

Blake was born in Soho in 1757 not far from his Poland Street house at 28 Broad Street, a corner house, now 74 Broadwick Street. Here, in a room above his father's hosiery shop, at the age of four he saw his first vision; the face of God looked in at the window and, not unnaturally, he screamed. By the time he was ten and going to drawing lessons in the Strand he was quite accustomed to seeing angels—once a tree full of them, their bright wings "bespangling every bough like stars." On hearing of that his father thought he should thrash him for a liar, but his mother intervened. His first published collection of lyrics was begun in his twelfth year.

At 41 Great Marlborough Street once lived the painter Benjamin

Benjamin Robert Haydon

Haydon. Never was anyone more dedicated to his art, never man had greater faith in his genius. He was unsparing of himself, his mother, his wife, his children and his friends in the cause. For him there was no compromise; he thought fit to insult all the Royal Academicians and would not stoop to paint pictures small enough to hang with convenience in ordinary private homes. Between 1822 (when he was thirty-six) and 1837 he was imprisoned for debt four times. And all the time he was absolutely mistaken. He had not a particle of genius. The best services he rendered to art were to encourage the national purchase of the Elgin marbles and the use of models in art schools, and to be the subject of a sonnet by Wordsworth and another by Keats.

Haydon was not without admiration in his own day. His success came early, flitted and never returned. In 1827 he wrote, "My *Judgment of Solomon* is rolled up in a warehouse in the Borough! My *Entry into Jerusalem*, once graced by the enthusiasm of the rank and beauty of the three kingdoms, is doubled up in a back room in Holborn! My *Lazarus* is in an upholsterer's shop in Mount Street! and my *Crucifixion* is in an hay-loft in Lisson Grove." There were still nineteen more years to go, in which to complete the twenty-six large MS. volumes of diary which he left behind him. In 1846 his *Banishment of Aristides*, the large fruit of long labour, was finished just when General Tom Thumb came to England. Both were shown in different sections of the Egyptian Hall. Haydon wrote: "Opened; rained hard; only Jerrold, Baring, Fox Maule and Hobhouse came. Rain would not have kept them away twenty-six years ago." Soon after: "They rush by thousands to see Tom Thumb. They push, they shout, they scream, they faint, they cry 'Help!' and 'Murder!' . . . It is an insanity, a furor, a dream. . . ." He killed himself 22nd June in his studio in front of one of his historical paintings.

Canaletto, who was twice in England, stayed at one time at 41 Beak Street, a house with a charming façade.

The most distinguished residents in Gerrard Street were Dryden (1631–1700), who spent his last four years at number 43, and Edmund Burke, who lodged at number 37 from 1787, when he was fifty-eight, till 1793, four years before he died. This was Burke's town house during the trial of Warren Hastings, whom he so wildly traduced. Burke's lengthy eloquence did not always show a sense of his audience; later he was known as "the dinner-bell" because when he spoke he regularly emptied the House of Commons. He once cut Fox in Dover Street, then eagerly asked his companion: "Did he look at me?" And he once said a very sensible thing to Mrs (afterwards Lady) Crewe; "A dull proser is more endurable than a dull joker."

From 1753 till 1761 Sir Joshua Reynolds lived at 5 Great Newport Street off Charing Cross Road. He then moved to 42 Leicester Square, now transformed, and stayed there till he died in 1792. In spite of his deafness he was extremely sociable, but never bothered with society etiquette in spite of being so fashionable a portrait painter. He was extremely peaceful and good-natured. Doctor Johnson and even sharp Mrs Thrale thought that no ill could be said of him. Samuel Rogers, however, repeats a friend's report that he found a girl crying on Sir Joshua's doorstep because, after she had posed all day, he had given her only a bad shilling and refused to change it.

Hogarth rose from poverty to a large house in the south-east corner of Leicester Square and a villa in Chiswick which he frequented less. His dog, his cat, his bullfinch are buried in the Chiswick garden. Hogarth when dying preferred 30 Leicester Square (then called Leicester Fields) and had himself carried back there, but he too is buried in Chiswick with an epitaph by Garrick. The last years of this genius were fretted and some say shortened by a bitter and public quarrel with his old friend the dissipated satirical poet Charles Churchill. Hogarth published a political print supporting Bute and ridiculing Pitt, Temple and Wilkes. Wilkes then published a violent attack on Hogarth in which he also sneered at the painter's wife. Hogarth therefore caricatured Wilkes in the court when he stood trial for high treason. When this was published, Churchill, a friend and partisan of Wilkes, wrote *An Epistle to William Hogarth* (1763) praising him as a great artist and attacking him as a man with vitriolic contempt, trying too to give him a push towards the grave by writing of him as in his dotage, tottering on its verge. Though Hogarth was a kind and high-minded man, he could be made fun of for self-esteem and self-importance. There was no fun in Churchill's *Epistle*. Garrick wrote him a moving letter begging him to refrain from publication till he saw him, but Churchill would not be turned aside. Hogarth came right back at him with a satire on his earlier connection with the Church, depicting him as a bear in tattered clerical bands with a pot of porter in one paw and a sheaf of lies and copies of Wilkes's paper in the other. But he was very deeply grieved and mortified. He died in October 1764, apparently cheerful towards the end, a few hours after beginning an answer to a letter from Benjamin Franklin.

Blake's first house with his bride was just off Leicester Square at 23 Green Street. He was there from 1782 till 1784.

Sir Isaac Newton had a house off Leicester Square at 35 St Martin's Street. His greatest work was done before he went there in 1720, but he spent the five happiest years of his life there—chiefly in the observatory. Among the lesser facts about him are that he was a seven-months child, that he studied alchemy, that he left a MS. work on the prophesies of Daniel and on the Apocalypse, a history of the Creation and several tracts. When Lamb was discussing at a party whom he would like to meet of the illustrious dead, he rejected Newton on the ground that he was simply "Principia," etc., but "n-not a person; not a p-person." Mildness, modesty and absence of mind may not make a man good company, but Newton had these qualities to so striking a degree that he was certainly a person. Few sayings are better known than his gentle and accurate remark to his dog on its destroying a manuscript, "Diamond, Diamond, thou knowst not what thou hast done." Once when he tried to lead a horse up a hill it was only at the very top that he discovered the animal had slipped its bridle and stayed below. He was often deceived as to whether or not he had eaten his dinner. When his cat and her kitten interrupted him ceaselessly to let them in and out of the room, he cut a hole in the wall of a suitable size for the cat and then he cut a smaller one for the kitten. It is naturally said of him that he once boiled his watch while looking at an egg for five minutes.

Later, Fanny Burney wrote *Evelina* in this same house.

His Majesty's Theatre in the Haymarket belonged at one time to Sir Beerbohm Tree (1853–1917). He took a great pride in it. Once when he kept exclaiming, "Look! Look at the 'House Full' boards outside my beautiful theatre!" someone pointed out that the Haymarket Theatre across the road had similar boards. "Ah," replied Tree, "but not so many."

The Haymarket Theatre (several times rebuilt) was for years associated with Samuel Foote. He was born in 1720, went to Oxford and on to the Temple without bothering to take a degree, and having squandered a fortune by the time he was twenty-four took to the stage as actor, dramatic author and director. He was not a good all-round actor but he was pre-eminently funny in his own pieces, remarkable for mimicry and libel. He introduced well-known living characters, including other actors such as Peg Woffington and Garrick. Garrick seems to have feared Foote and was certainly very amiable to him, constantly lending him money and always being mocked for parsimony. Foote had remarkably little trouble with his victims. After his play *The Nabob* two members of the East India Company called to beat him up, but he met them with such tact and charm that they stayed for a friendly dinner. Doctor Johnson stood up to him, and successfully. On hearing that he was to be caricatured, he sent word that "he would go from the boxes to the stage and there correct him in front of the audience"; Foote chose discretion. But Johnson left this record of him:

> "The first time I was in company with Foote was at Fitzherbert's. Having no good opinion of the fellow I was resolved not to be pleased, and it is very difficult to please a man against his will. I went on eating my dinner pretty sullenly, affecting not to mind him. But the dog was so very comical that I was obliged to lay down my knife and fork, throw myself back upon my chair, and fairly laugh it out. No, sir, he was irresistible."

Fox told Rogers of meeting him at a party of Lord William Bentinck's where all expected him to be tiresome and all were delighted by him, finding his talk brilliant on no matter what subject.

He was short, fat, flabby, intelligent-looking with very bright eyes. He was greedy and selfish and had so few redeeming traits that when any appeared they shone like virtues by contrast. Perhaps it counts as a redeeming trait that he took his accident so well. He was on a visit to Lord Mexborough in 1766 and an aristocratic party, including the Duke of York, lured him through his vanity on to a dangerous horse. It threw him and broke his leg in two places. He behaved very calmly; and when the doctor decided on amputation his comment was: "Now I shall be able to take off old Faulkner to the life." The Duke of York got him a patent worth a fortune to erect a theatre in Westminster and exhibit dramatic pieces every summer as long as he lived.

He lived another eleven years, and he did get into trouble in the end. The Duchess of Kingston, against whom a suit for bigamy was pending, heard (for he always talked too much) that she was to be libelled as Lady Kitty Crocodile in *The Trip to Calais*. She got the piece prohibited. Foote offered various excisions and alterations, but she would not compromise; so he said if the play could not be played it could be published and dedicated to her. She then called in Parson Jackson, a notorious Irish adventurer, to attack him in the gutter news-sheets. Foote offered to abstain from publication if the attacks were called off. The Duchess then sent a belligerent letter, which Foote answered with an insolence and wit which turned all laughs against her. Moreover, he recast *The Trip to Calais* as *The Capuchin* and pilloried Parson Jackson as Doctor Viper. The Duchess wrote a scandalous letter to the *Evening Post* and Jackson suborned an ex-coachman of Foote's to support a groundless charge of unnatural vice. This really broke Foote. The jury acquitted him without leaving the box, but he gave up the theatre and died, bequeathing his money to his two illegitimate sons. Horace Walpole conjectured that the Duchess—who was unduchessed by being convicted of bigamy—would leave her possessions to three co-heiresses: the Empress of Russia, Lady Salisbury and the whore of Babylon. In fact, she left a very complicated, rambling will behind, when she died of breaking a blood-vessel from rage in 1788—eleven years after the death of Foote. She was bravely swigging Madeira to the last gasp.

The Haymarket was the centre of the gilded vice and gaiety district in the 1860's. In the Haymarket itself were The Burmese, The Blue Posts, Barnes's and Barron's Oyster Rooms. The dancing-rooms of the fat and famous Kate Hamilton had a long, tunnel-like entry from south-east Coventry Street, and extended back to Leicester Square. The place was regularly raided by the police, who loitered politely in the tunnel while bottles and glasses were hidden under floor boards. No ambitious young dog felt he was anybody till Kate's deep, raucous voice had summoned him to her side and given him leave to buy champagne for everyone. In Panton Street were Jack Percival's and Rose Burton's, and houses of ill-fame for every vice. The famous Argyll Rooms, a great drinking and dancing resort, stood where the Trocadero later rose. A much lower grade dancing-saloon, the Pic, was replaced by the Criterion. There were rows and smashed hats and bleeding noses every night at the Pic, and such things were not unknown at the smart Café Riche which adjoined it. Other superior haunts were the Clarendon Restaurant in Bond Street and Mott's in Foley Street—where Freer, the proprietor, would welcome any man of birth and position, no matter how dissolute, but reject the wealthiest and most respectable parvenus. The resorts were open all night and blazed with lights till morning.

Joseph Hardman records the difficulty he had, after a good dinner, in dragging his young friend Meredith, who was staying with him, home past the Haymarket—he was "so very rampant."

The Marquis of Hastings, a great one for playing practical jokes and for standing treat all round in pubs, was a terrific night-life king. The night-life queens were not from the aristocracy—though Shoes, for example, married into it. Among them were Skittles and Sweet Nelly Fowler, Nelly Clifford, Baby Jordan and so on.

On one occasion Lord Hastings went to Windmill Street off Shaftesbury Avenue for a bag of two hundred lively sewer rats, provided by Jimmy Shaw, a professional catcher who spent half the day hunting in the main drains. The purchase was nothing out of the way to Jimmy. He supplied rats in bulk every night to various sporting haunts, plunging his hand into a sack of the savage beasts and counting them out to be pitted against ferrets or for the young bloods to try dogs on—a dog might be backed to kill a thousand. Jimmy would have Cabinet Ministers and peers and army men throwing him sovereigns as he pulled out his captures by their tails. He handed over the bag to Lord Hastings, who, being very well known for his larks, insisted that his innocent-faced friend Bobby Shafto should carry it under his cloak. The sporting haunt to which they went was Mott's octagon ballroom, with the glass dome and the brilliant gas lighting. Proprietor Freer urged good behaviour, as Lord Londesborough was giving a supper-party for his reigning favourite, attended by no end of toffs. Up they came from supper to the ballroom, two hundred men and women in a room of forty by thirty feet, where they were swiftly plunged into total darkness and joined by two hundred sewer rats. Hastings and Shafto vanished to Cremorne, where you could count on a fast time and a few rows.

The particular heroine of Lord Londesborough's supper-party was Sweet Nelly Fowler. Her prefix was not a compliment to her character, but to an unusual phenomenon. It was admitted on all sides that this beautiful girl had an exquisite natural perfume. It was so much admired that men paid large sums in order to have their handkerchiefs placed under her pillow when she slept. This, it seems, was enough to scent them most charmingly. And so it was no unusual thing to find the odour of Miss Fowler wafted about in the most respectable, exclusive London drawing-rooms.

VIII

The West End; St. James's, Mayfair, Piccadilly, etcetera

The Mall is haunted by the ghost of poor Otway, waiting, waiting, looking in vain for a glimpse of Mrs Barry. For the beautiful actress who was Rochester's mistress, who was kind and helpful to her young rival Mrs Bracegirdle, for whom Otway wrote so many parts and whom he loved so dearly, so unwisely and so long, gave him an appointment there which she did not keep. He was the more unhappy because she had charged him with some wrong which he denied, in torment and suspense till she would acquit him. "You were pleased to send me word that you would meet me in the Mall this evening, and give me further satisfaction in the matter you were so unkind to charge me with; I was there, but found you not." It is the last of the six letters which remain of the many he may have written her, and we learn no more of his loving.

Gainsborough lived at 80 Pall Mall, and it was in this street that Wycherley, in the first flush of success and the heyday of good looks and youth, was accosted so brazenly by Barbara Duchess of Cleveland.

Gladstone passed some time at 11 Carlton House Terrace, and also at 10 St James's Square, which commemorates too William Pitt, Earl of Chatham, and the Earl of Derby. Gladstone stands out among so many lamentable histories as having had a happy life and a noble reach of mind. In his view, he and Queen Victoria finally jogged along fairly well together. He described this relationship in terms of an expedition he had once made abroad with friends. There was a serviceable but displeasing and difficult pack-mule whom the party had found it impossible to love. By the end it had done a good job and they had some value and respect for it, though it was still strictly unlovable. As this mule, said Gladstone, was he to Queen Victoria.

Sir Isaac Newton once lived in Jermyn Street at number 87.

Edmund Waller had a house in St James's Street. He was of no value as a critic; he generally praised everything contemporary from good-nature, and he opined that *Paradise Lost* was remarkable only for its length. His own best-known poems, the faultless lyric *Go, lovely rose* and the moving lines on old age, are brief enough. He was a man not only of wit but of great charm; he was enormously liked, and his transgressions were always forgiven. He did not come very well out of the unsuccessful plot to seize London for Charles I in 1643, but it does not appear that he bore false witness against others in struggling for his own life. His retort when Charles II asked him why his verses of welcome to himself were so inferior to his eulogy of Cromwell may pass as witty, "Sir, we poets never succeed so well in writing truth as in fiction." His retort when he met again in later years his admired Sacharissa (Lady Dorothy Sidney, then Dowager Countess of Sunderland) will not pass at all. She rashly asked, "When, Mr Waller, when, I wonder, will you write such beautiful verses to me again!" "When, madam, your ladyship is as young and as handsome again," said Ned Waller, usually a courteous and gallant man. Men of many nationalities found him delightful company, and he was affectionate. His first marriage was mercenary, but he did grieve for the lady's early death, and most deeply mourned his beautiful second wife. He fought hard in the House of Commons for toleration of Quakers and other dissenters, saying that he had "a sense of kindness for any persons that suffer," and that he would not have "the Church of England, like the elder brother of the Ottoman family, strangle all the younger brothers."

One of Colonel Blood's famous escapades took place in St James's Street in 1670. The Duke of Ormonde, his particular enemy from old days in Ireland and a dignified misfit at the parvenu court, was driving back to Clarendon House, Piccadilly, from an entertainment for the visiting Prince of Orange. Blood and five accomplices seized him from his coach with intent to murder. There was nothing to prevent the murder had not the Colonel been taken with the fancy to hang the Duke at Tyburn. He rode ahead to fix the rope, whereat the old man put up such a good fight against the understrappers that he held up their progress till rescue arrived. Next year, when Charles II pardoned Colonel Blood's equally nearly successful attempt to steal the regalia from the Tower, he sent a courteous request or demand for the Duke of Ormonde's agreement. The Duke obligingly replied that it was far from him to value his life more than the King valued his crown.

At 22 St James's Place, overlooking the park, lived Samuel Rogers who knew everyone (who was Anyone) and is more noted now for his

Table Talk than for his poetry. One of the anecdotes in *Table Talk* concludes with a sage and undeniable reflection:

> "When a lady, a friend of mine, was in Italy, she went into a church, and knelt down among the crowd. An Italian woman, who was praying at some little distance, rose up, came softly to my friend, whispered in her ear, 'If you continue to flirt with my husband, I'll be the death of you'; and then, as softly, returned to her genuflections. Such things cannot happen where there are pews."

Sir Robert Walpole lived at 5 Arlington Street.

Charles James Fox (1749–1806) lived at 9 Arlington Street. It would have been intolerable if a man so self-indulgent, extravagant and careless with money, had not been generous with it; he was also essentially, generous-minded. Financial recklessness and inefficiency did not bring the usual tale of misery. In him was a real capacity for enjoyment and he had an enjoyable life. He had many interests other than politics, gambling, drinking and good company. For example, he was an excellent classical scholar. Euripedes was a great favourite with him, and he read Homer every year, the *Odyssey* with more pleasure than the *Iliad*, although he ranked the *Iliad* higher. One of the aphorisms which he liked, from Hippocrates, is worth remembrance and application: "The second-best remedy is better than the best, if the patient likes it best." He showed great good judgment in marrying his mistress Mrs Armistead, a refined ex-courtesan with whom he was happy and who cherished him devotedly. Rogers when breakfasting with them once had the misfortune to make a gaffe; he broke into praise of Goldsmith's song *When lovely woman stoops to folly*. Mrs Fox was much discomposed, but Fox merely said, "Some people write damned nonsense." He loved his many friends, and no man was better beloved in return than he. It was typical of the deep feeling his friends had for him that years after his death one of them, Sir Robert Adair, on learning that he was in the room at Chiswick House in which Fox had died, burst into a passion of tears.

Crossing to the north side of Piccadilly, it will be convenient to track the lost denizens of Mayfair in a zig-zag course from Park Lane to Regent Street, ending the London tour with the length of Piccadilly itself from Albany to Apsley House—"No. 1 London."

Edward Jenner (1749–1823), originator of vaccination, lived at 4 Park Lane and at 14 Hertford Street.

Skittles, perhaps the most famous demi-mondaine of the sixties,

"Skittles"

lived at 15 South Street. This was not in her heyday, but from 1882 till her death in 1920 at the age of eighty-one. She was then known as Mrs Baillie, but Mrs was an honorary title. She never married, though at one time in Paris she was held to cherish hopes of marrying Lord Hartington and becoming in due course a duchess. Lord Clanricarde was another great friend of early days. Like Laura Bell she was not lonely and neglected in her old age, but had a wide circle of friends. Among them were Edward VII and Kitchener, who valued her good-humour and wit. She had a vivid interest in life to the last, and was planning an aeroplane trip a few days before her death.

Again like Laura Bell, she created a furor in her youth driving her smart ponies in Hyde Park, pulling up in due course to hold court near the Achilles statue, while great ladies and their daughters in high barouches drove by with contemptuous glances, angry bridling or pretended unawareness. The equestrian fashion was still in full swing, and all her friends and rivals would also ride and drive in the fashionable hours.

> The pretty little horse-breakers
> Are breaking hearts like fun,
> For in Rotten Row they all must go
> The whole hog or none,

says a music-hall song of the period. *The Times* of 3rd July 1862 carried a long letter about her signed H. and attributed to Higgins ("Jacob Omnium"):

"Early in the season 1861 a young lady whom I must call Anonyma, for I have never been able to learn her name, made her appearance in Hyde Park. She was a charming creature, beautifully dressed, and she drove with ease and spirit two of the handsomest brown ponies eye ever beheld. . . . A good many young gentlemen seem to be acquainted with her. . . . Driving becomes the rage. Three to six hundred guineas were given for pairs of ponies on condition they should be as handsome as Anonyma's. . . . She threads her way dexterously, with an unconscious air, through the throng, commented on by hundreds who admire and hundreds who envy her. She pulls up her ponies to speak to an acquaintance, and her carriage is instantly surrounded by a multitude. . . . Meanwhile, thousands returning from the Exhibition are intolerably delayed by the crowd collected to gaze on this pretty creature and her pretty ponies, and the efforts of Sir Richard Mayne and his police to keep the thoroughfare open are utterly frustrated."

She was born in 1839 in Liverpool. One version of her nickname is that in childhood and adolescence she was in charge of the Skittle Alley at the Black-Jack Tavern. Another is that, being in liquor, she bawled at some Guardsmen who were chaffing her that "If they didn't hold their bloody row, she'd knock them down like a row of bloody skittles!" *Mémoires d'une Biche Anglaise*, the French translation of *Skittles, a Biography of a Fascinating Woman*, renders the name as Quillette, from *le jeu de quilles*; she was certainly known as Skitsie in part of her Paris career. Her real name was probably Catherine Walters, though in the flood of books purporting to be authentic histories of her and other equestrian courtesans she is sometimes called Caroline Walters or Waters. *Une Autre Biche Anglaise* states that the nickname Anonyma really belonged to another courtesan. She was known in New York as well as in London and Paris, bolting there in 1862 with a Mr Aubrey de Vere Beauclerk, with whom she stayed till the following year. He left behind young children and a charming wife, who thought he would return to her and patiently waited thirty years to divorce him. He had previously been engaged to a girl in Ireland, but had absented himself without explanation on the wedding-day. Her sixteen-year-old brother pursued him to his London club and thrashed him with a stout blackthorn stick.

Skittles did not merely drive; she was a magnificent rider and hunted hard in Leicestershire. This may be why the society ladies who explored her luxuriously decorated house in Chesterfield Street, up for sale on her New York elopement, found to their fascination that she had put in a padded swansdown lavatory seat.

Of the famous people who lived in Clarges Street, Sir William and Lady Hamilton (Number 11) and Macaulay (Number 3) will be met with again in Piccadilly. Edmund Kean, who made his stage début as a cupid when he was four, lived at Number 12.

Kean's life hardly bears thinking of. Its latter years are the more intolerably poignant because at one time it was the most magnificent of true Cinderella stories. The death of a beloved elder child while he and his wife Mary were abjectly poor at Dorchester, their wretched suspense also over a muddle between two rival engagements for the all-important London début, are starker than the cinders and the crusts. His character too was stormy and proud and sombre, in contrast to the glad sweetness of the dear girl with the ugly sisters. But the miserable arrival in London in one of the most ferocious winters, the anxious pillar-to-posting between the two affronted and elusive managers, the scornful unkindness of the actors at Theatre Royal, Drury Lane, before and after a verbal contract was at length settled, the efforts to dissuade him—twenty-six years old and only five feet five inches tall, with a large head—from the risk of opening in the great rôle of Shylock, the adverse criticism at the ill-attended and only rehearsal, the cold hostility back-stage and the sparse audience in front which greeted him on the night itself, were indeed a dramatic build-up for the glory of 26th January 1814. As Buttons befriended Cinderella, so did one person befriend the Keans through this anguish. Miss Williams, their landlady at 21 Cecil Street, Strand, had compassion and faith; she let them stay on owing her their rent. And the godfather of Kean's triumph was the good friend who had recommended him to the Drury Lane Theatre—himself named Doctor Drury.

Mary, no Princess Charming anyway, had to be at home with little Charles in his cot, but Miss Williams and Doctor Drury were in front; so were Hazlitt and Douglas Jerrold. The house was about a third full, but it sounded like a full house as applause swelled for Kean. For the second act it was indeed much fuller; in the interval people had dragged their friends in from coffee-houses and even from Covent Garden Theatre. When the play was over Kean fled home, pausing only to speak to Doctor Drury. He caught his wife in his arms—"You shall ride in your carriage, Mary, and you, Charles, shall go to Eton."

The management were now anxious about their omission to give and secure a written contract. So high was Kean's sudden leap to fame that he could well have gone back on them. But his honour and pride induced him to sign to the original agreement for eight guineas a week. Then they tore it up and produced a contract for twenty and a present of fifty pounds. Kean could now be generous to his friends (he was very generous) and slight his enemies. He even slighted some who were not his enemies, such as Byron, simply through preferring the company of pugilists and pot-house Bohemians to that of lords. He took a pet lion-cub with him everywhere; he indulged his vanity; he indulged his love for brandy. But still his triumphant mastery of his art increased, and still he was settled with Mary and his child. A contemporary print shows him as Richard III carrying Drury Lane Theatre on his back; it was true enough. He opened his third season, 12th January 1816, as Sir Giles Overreach in Massinger's *A New Way to Pay Old Debts*. It was terrific. Women screamed, Byron was terrified, the leading lady fainted. The audience roared for him at the end as no audience had ever done even for Garrick. Once more he rushed back to his wife, now at 12 Clarges Street. "I've done it again, Mary," he cried. She asked, "And what did Lord Essex think of it?" Kean said, "Damn Lord Essex. The pit rose at me."

It all happened. The glory was real and immortal. The good years were no more a dream than the long-drawn evils to follow. Kean lost health and credit through drink. The public knew what it meant when he was too "ill" to appear, and though he could win them back he learned what it was to face an angry audience. By 1821 he was desperately taken up with the bottle—and with Charlotte Cox, the temperamental wife of an alderman. In 1825 Alderman Cox won a suit against the actor for adultery with his wife, and press and public were bitter against Kean. There were attempts to howl him off the stage for ever, but he faced the furious mob bravely and he won through against the teeth of his enemies. When the season and a tour were over he went for a year to North America (where he was made Chief of a Red Indian tribe). He got a great welcome back; and worked hard, for his money had gone. Physically he was greatly worn, a far cry from the young man who had once been a wonderful dancer and an excellent harlequin. His mind too was impaired by his irregularities; he could no longer learn new parts. He tried to in 1827 with his friend Grattan's *Ben Nazir* (they found him weeping in his dressing-room when his entrance was almost due) and in 1830 with *Henry V*; he stumbled and mumbled through both incomprehensibly, cutting wildly and quite lost, the first to a hostile house, the second to an audience of merciless tigers. Gone was his never very happy marriage; he and Mary were living apart. He had quarrelled with his son, though not for ever. It remained that he was a fighter. Crippled with the gout and broken with the brandy, within a year of his death he summoned force and fire and technique to outplay the rising Macready. He was playing Othello at Covent Garden in March 1833 when his last illness struck him. He died some six weeks later, aged forty-five. Mary had had her carriage and Charles had gone to Eton; but missing from the story were the words "they lived happily ever after."

Benjamin Disraeli, Earl of Beaconsfield, died at 19 Curzon Street. Lady Mary Wortley Montagu once resided at No. 15.

Beau Brummell, who lived at 42 Charles Street, we shall meet at another establishment.

Horace Walpole's London house from 1779 till his death in 1797 was 40 (now 11) Berkeley Square. The long correspondence with Mme du Deffand had still a year to run, and some of her interesting, pitiable letters must have come to this house as well as to Strawberry Hill out at Twickenham. Walpole was on the whole a kindly man, enthusiastic in admiration, sharp and often prejudiced but not bitter in enmity, constant in friendship. He gave no help to Chatterton, "the marvellous boy who perished in his pride" for lack of it, but Chatterton was a stranger who had sent him forgeries. He provided for that charming woman Kitty Clive, actress and singer:

("All I ask of any man
Is to love me while he can,"

was the reasonable sentiment of one of her popular songs) and for the well-liked Berry sisters, Agnes and Mary. For fifteen years he and the stone-blind Mme du Deffand, twenty years his senior, wrote to each other about once a week, except when he was in Paris and regularly seeing her. He was really attached to her and a great admirer of her wit and her wits; but it was good of him to write so often, though he did remonstrate and even scold, for to her it was a romantic friendship and she wrote to him with a girl's ardour. Any man was bound to chafe at the absurdity, however touching; Walpole, satirical and witty himself, was particularly nervous lest she and his letters to her should make him ridiculous.

Walpole was forty-eight when he went to Paris and met a typical set of Louis XV ladies, all of them leading or having led lives of gallantry, all very serious upholders of wit and atheism. Mme de Talmond, said to have been the mistress of Charles Edward Stuart, had affected religion to please the Queen, and wore a pair of bracelets one with a picture of the Young Pretender and the other with a picture of Our Lord; asked for the connection between them she replied, "Their kingdoms are not of this world." Mme du Deffand, who had always been a sceptic, originated a proverb with her very just and sincerely spoken reply to a credulous ecclesiastic. He explained to her at what places St Denis had stopped to rest when walking with his head under his arm from Ouen, the place of his martyrdom by decapitation, to the suburb of Paris named after him. When he added that the first stage of progress had been the most taxing, "Ah," she cried, "I can well believe that, for in affairs of that kind, *ce n'est que le premier pas qui coûte.*"

On her death Walpole, as she had wished, adopted her beloved and notoriously disagreeable dog Ton-ton, had indeed asked to do so on the ground that it was "so cross that nobody else would treat it well." He was soon rewarded by finding he adored the creature; how much he missed the long habit of its mistress's friendship we do not know. "You will regret me," she guessed in her last letter, "because it is pleasant to feel that one is loved."

At 15 Grosvenor Square, the house of Mr Thistlethwayte and his wife, née Laura Bell, there was a curious accident on 9th August 1887, when the couple had been married for thirty-five years and she, aged fifty-eight, had long been a penitent evangelist. It was Mr Thistlethwayte's custom to keep a loaded revolver by his bed. He is supposed to have fainted, fallen, overturned the table, and caused the revolver to go off at him with impeccable and fatal aim.

William Blake with his wife Catherine lived at 17 South Moulton Street from 1803 to 1821 in two rooms on the first floor. There he was visited by Mahomet, Moses, Julius Caesar, David and Bathsheba and many other distinguished spirits who came to sit for their portraits. Contemporary visitors would see him turn aside from his painting to look searchingly at features invisible to them.

Nelson lived at 147 New Bond Street.

At 47A in the same road, at the corner of Maddox Street (where her house was), Madame Rachel in 1863 opened a small shop over which was written in gilt "Beautiful for Ever." Her range of tints in cosmetics was certainly a great improvement on the earlier pearl powder and red paint, and as there was nothing in the shop under a guinea—a mere tablet of alluringly named soap cost two guineas—she did well enough out of these. But a more important line of business was remedial treatment. A course of Arabian baths (made from ordinary hot water and bran, as was later proved) cost from fifty pounds to five hundred guineas, and it cost a thousand guineas to have the whole works. Dissatisfied customers of this pioneer salon could not easily complain, as in those days to seek artificial aid to beauty was condemned as ridiculous and, moreover, highly improper and sinful. Madam Rachel, large, hideous and formidable, did not stop at pointing this out when threatened with exposure; she would threaten on her side to assert that the cheated woman had kept assignations with men at the shop. She even robbed one client of her jewels with impunity. She amassed considerable wealth, and had she stuck to her ordinary line of extortion and blackmail might have had an entirely triumphant career. Her rapacity undid her. In 1867 she met the once-pretty and eternally silly Widow Borrodaile. When this woman had spent all her ready money on treatment, Madame Rachel informed her that Lord Ranelagh had spied on her in the beauty bath through a chink, had fallen in love, and would in due course marry her if she would leave the entire conduct of the affair in Madame's hands. Mrs Borrodaile's extreme gullibility, her acceptance of vulgar letters dictated to the errand boy as coming from her noble conquest, her readiness to be defrauded of all her capital, seem to have aroused hatred in her persecutor. Persistent and outrageous acquiescence from the victim might well disgust a criminal. The first "bride" whom Smith murdered was the one to whom he had wantonly written a false accusation of having a venereal disease after robbing and stranding her, and who eagerly went straight back to him when they met again by accident. At any rate, Madame Rachel could not stop till she had robbed Mrs Borrodaile of every penny she had, stripped her house of valuables, and had her in prison for debt. The widow was not on terms with any of her relations, but they found out what had happened and Madame Rachel was brought to trial.

Mrs Borrodaile's ordeal was a wretched one. Lord Ranelagh himself was there, joining in the roars of laughter in court at the enamelled figure of fun. *The Times* report called her a "senescent Sappho." One can only hope that she felt more or less dazed.

Madame was sentenced to five years' penal servitude, served four, started up again in business, and was doing well all over again when excessive rapacity again brought her into court. She died in prison.

Canning lived at 37 Conduit Street, and once made a joke of which Tom Moore said that "the person who does not relish it can have no perception of real wit." A lady foolishly asked him, "Why have they made the spaces in the iron gate of Spring Gardens so narrow?" Canning replied, "Oh, ma'am, because such very fat people used to go through."

Lady Mary Wortley Montagu died in 1762 at a house in Hanover Square. She had married for love, eloping to escape a detested rich match, and though her marriage ended in an amicable separation bridged by pleasant correspondence, it had some happy years, started her famous travels, and was by no means wretched. She had her share of faults, follies and troubles; and her summing up of life on her deathbed, so moderate yet so satisfactory, was particularly heartening, as many of us may be able to say as much. "Well, it's all been very interesting," were the last words of Lady Mary.

Colonel Francis Charteris moved from Poland Street to George Street, Hanover Square, and his wife went to the country, after their daughter's marriage in 1720. Gambling and lending money on land

Lady Mary Wortley Montagu

and general sharp practice had made him a very rich man; when he was dying he repeatedly offered £30,000 to anyone who would convince him that hell did not exist, but the reward was not claimed. The George Street house was soon infamous throughout London, so procuresses, Mother Needham among them, were employed to bring good-looking girls arriving in London from the provinces as domestic servants. Unless specially favoured (one was allowed to have three children by him) they were turned out unprovided for after a few days. There were stories current of girls seduced at the point of a pistol and of more than Roman orgies; and the Colonel was hated by the populace. Remarkable as was his ravenous appetite for relays of women, he was almost equally notorious both for ill-gotten wealth and for meanness. Arbuthnot published an epitaph on his death in 1732 at the age of fifty-seven as one "who with an inflexible constancy, and inimitable uniformity of life, persisted in spite of age and infirmity in the practice of every human vice, excepting prodigality and hypocrisy; his insatiable avarice exempting him from the first, and his matchless impudence from the second." His hearse was pelted with garbage, there was an attempt to tear him from his coffin, and dead dogs and cats were flung in his grave. Nevertheless he was not friendless. When the grossly treated Ann Bond brought a charge against him and he stood trial for rape in 1730 in peril of condemnation to death, such men as the Duke of Argyll, James Bruce and Robert Walpole were active in helping to procure him a pardon. Swift, who was not his friend, assured Pope that there were many old villains and monsters in Dublin more wicked and stupid than Charteris. It is only fair to point out that one of his few recorded acts of generosity had met with discouragement. Grateful for a fine of only £80 after biting off a miller's nose, he proffered £10 to the judges for drinks and was fined another £50 for contempt of court.

Sheridan died in 1816 at 14 Savile Row, and might have died in a sponging-house but for his physician's strong line with the sheriff's officer and an eleventh-hour present from his latterly neglectful society friends. He had been dragged to a sponging-house once already, bitterly wounded at such profanation of his person. Financial distresses had piled up upon him during his year in Savile Row. The house is a charming one; still a most elegant place, for it is now Hardy Amies, the establishment of one of the great dress designers. One cannot think that Sheridan and "Hecca," his second wife, were very happy there. In that house he spoke his last words, "I am utterly undone"; from that house he sent his last message to Lady Bessborough, that his eyes (of which he was vain) would look up to the coffin-lid as brightly as ever.

Rogers said that "in his dealings with the world, Sheridan certainly carried the *privileges of genius* as far as they were ever carried by man." He persecuted his good friend Lady Bessborough most woefully with a passion which for years she tried to reject with kindness only; if it is true that he was the author of the filthy poison-pen letters with illustrations which came to her and even to her daughter, it was carrying the privileges of genius and of tormented love very far indeed. If it is true, then he has got away even with that, for posterity forgives him everything, including absorption in politics, so that he wrote nothing after *The Critic* and *Pizzaro* in 1779, except a pantomime called *Robinson Crusoe or Harlequin Friday*. His romantic elopement with the lovely, accomplished Miss Linley, his warmth of heart, his brilliance of wit, his reckless imprudence, all endear. There is something appealing about a man who uses banknotes to stuff up rattling windows; who goes on the principle that if you don't open letters they'll answer themselves in time; who has to be locked up with wine and sandwiches, pen and paper, if his last act is to be finished in time for his first night; who leaves the carefully prepared notes of an important speech behind him and then is better extempore; who discharges large liabilities not properly his own, and, unable to pay his ordinary debts, domesticates the bailiffs. Sheridan meant to pay his debts, and had great financial misfortunes other than his own extravagance. But drink and irresponsibility with money led to much that was sad and sordid. In his decline he became quarrelsome, maudlin and morose. But in his decline Byron said of him, and stuck to it, "His very dregs are better than 'the first sprightly runnings' of others."

Albany, at the Circus end of Piccadilly, was the house of the Melbournes, Caroline Lamb's in-laws, before they exchanged it with the Duke of York for his mansion in Whitehall. Byron is associated with it out of all proportion considering that he only lived there, at A2 (later taken by Bulwer Lytton), for one year. He arrived 28th March 1814. He would get drunk at the Cocoa Tree at 64 St James's Street and then live for days on biscuits and soda water. He practised the broadsword and for an hour every day he boxed. Lady Caroline Lamb came to his chambers at least twice. On the first known occasion she was characteristically disguised as a page, and penetrated undeterred by the news that he was out. When Byron came back to find "Remember me" scrawled in her hand on the fly leaf of an open book, he flew into a rage at the thought of her prowling among his private possessions. He wrote;

Remember thee—remember thee!
Till Lethe quench life's burning stream
Remorse and shame shall cling to thee,
And haunt thee like a feverish dream.
Remember thee! Ay, doubt it not,
Thy husband too shall think of thee,
By neither shalt thou be forgot,
Thou false to him, thou fiend to me!

But he was softened in her actual presence the last time she came. She had charm, she had been constant in devotion for three years, he may well have felt that few had real affection for him, and he knew that society was turning against him—and would turn further. It was natural that he should confide in her; "he had showed me letters and told me things I cannot repeat." At parting he pressed his lips to hers and said, "Poor Caro, if everyone hates me, you will, I see, never change—no, not even with ill-usage." She answered, "Yes, I *am* changed, and shall come near you no more." They never saw each other alone again.

March 1815 saw Byron married and established at 139 Piccadilly, then 13 Piccadilly Terrace, where Coleridge read him *Kubla Khan*. On his marriage night, Byron waked suddenly from his first sleep into a red glare, cast through the crimson bed-curtains by a taper left burning in the room. "Good God, I am surely in hell!" he cried, loudly enough to wake his bride.

Macaulay moved to E1 Albany in 1840. After one of his breakfast parties there the guests insisted, in spite of his pooh-poohing, on trying table-turning with a very solid, heavy table. The opinions rapped out by tables afford no especially reliable guidance, but tables burst into movement under the touch of a circle of contacting fingers and thumbs. This one did so. Macaulay was much disconcerted when all denied pushing it, till Bishop Wilberforce, known as Soapy Sam, kindly said perhaps he might have given it a slight unconscious shove.

Macaulay was a most formidable and relentless talker. Even as a small child, when his mother commented impatiently upon some minor mishap, he replied, as aptly as impressively, "Madam, it is part of that vast scheme of annoyance which governs this sublunary sphere."

Burlington House was a great centre of Whig hospitality in the third Earl of Burlington's day. He was indeed a splendid host; Handel stayed with him for three years and the architect William Kent for thirty-two. His wife's favourite protegée was la Violetta, the dancer who delighted London and won Garrick for ever by her "gaiety with innocence."

Clarendon House was next door to Devonshire House, and built a year earlier, fronting St James's Street and St James's Palace. Edward Hyde, Earl of Clarendon, was a great man when he built it: Lord Chancellor, still an influence on Charles II, his daughter married to the heir-apparent. (In fact, this marriage had vexed him greatly and brought him irrational public blame for the Queen's sterility. "He looks to be the gandfather of kings, curse him.") He built a grandiose upstart palace, beginning in 1664 with stones intended to repair old St Paul's. Morals were later turned on those stones stolen from God, and indeed it could have been aptly quoted, "Except the Lord build the house their labour is but lost that build it." Charles was already tiring of Clarendon and chafing under him, and the mob hated him. In 1667 the Dutch sailed up Gravesend. The people called his house Dunkirk House, to suggest he'd been bribed to sell it, and Tangier House, to deride as valueless his aquisition of Tangier for England. Pepys wrote, "They have cut down the trees before his house and broke his windows; and a gibbet either set up before or painted upon his gate, and these words writ: 'Three sights to be seen,—Dunkerke, Tangier and a barren Queen.'" He had opposed the marriage and was not a gynaecologist, but Rochester, defied by Charles to find a rhyme for Lisbon, improvised

> Here's health to Kate
> Our Sovereign's mate,
> Of the Royal House of Lisbon:
> But the devil take Hyde,
> And the Bishop beside,
> Who made her bone of his bone.

The workmen were not out of Clarendon House when the Great Seal was demanded of its owner. Desolate and crippled with gout, he waited in his chair for the impeachment for high treason. He appealed piteously to the King, and the King hardened his heart and sent him to France. He died, an exile, seven years after.

Clarendon's sons leased the house to the second Duke of Ormonde, a grand old man of earlier fashions, whom Colonel Blood attacked in St James's Street. Its next owner, the Duke of Albermarle, was a wastrel and a drunkard. He sold it to a syndicate who pulled it down within twenty years of its building.

Devonshire House stood where now is the large motor-car emporium of Messrs Rootes.

So much has been written, so much has been written well, of Devonshire House when William the fifth duke lived there with his beautiful and spirited duchess, who had been Lady Georgiana Spencer, that it is well to be brief here. The calm, conventional Duke makes little appeal to imagination. The Duchess was the most generous, simple, rash and charming of great Whig hostesses. Nothing is better known about her than that, when canvassing for her friend Charles James Fox in the Westminster Election of 1784, she entered "some of the most blackguard houses in the Long Acre," bought a butcher's vote with a kiss, and was told by an Irish mechanic that he could light his pipe at her eyes. (G. S. Street in his *Ghosts of Piccadilly* asks female readers to decide whether they would prefer to have that compliment paid them, or Richard Steele's to another woman—that to love her was a liberal education.) Georgiana was wilder and more impulsive than that greatest of all her many friends, her younger sister Harriet, who married Lord Duncannon and on her father-in-law's death became Lady Bessborough. A less likely lifelong friend for her, at first consideration, was Lady Elizabeth Foster, whom she introduced into her household and who became the Duke of Devonshire's permanent and resident mistress, succeeding her as Duchess after her death in 1806. In fact, Georgiana had no cause to regret her generosity in importing Bess. Her husband was the one man whom she feared and to whom she did not know how to talk. There was nothing jealous or grudging in her nature, and the fact that her friend amused and pleased her husband certainly made life more comfortable. It was Bess who at last tackled the Duke for her about the wretched gambling debts which so preyed upon her mind and health, and who saw to it that all were paid. Lady Elizabeth Foster was not as lovable a character as the two sisters, but her gratitude and affection to Georgiana was never in doubt, and it is to her credit that Harriet—cleverer, deeper and more critical than her elder sister—was also her friend. The women understood each other.

The brilliant Spencer sisters, Georgiana and Harriet, were tremendous magnets to men, had deep friendships, likings and loves among them, besides flirtations, and enjoyed masculine company. Like all attractive women, they were charmed by potential rivals, their sympathies were aroused by other attractive women, they were melted by beauty, delighted by wit and bound by tenderness of heart in their own sex. They were unusual not in kind but in degree. The enthusiasm, honesty and constancy of their attachments to friends male or female were unsurpassed. When the Duchess died Fox said that they had lost the warmest heart in England. Their warmth and generosity were matched by their unworldliness. The imprudent elder sister and the clever critical younger sister had not an ounce of calculation, snobbery or materialism between them. With enormous capacity for enjoyment in this world, they lived for the things of the heart and the spirit. And for all their independence and dash, they had humility; they grieved for their follies and sins; they tried to do better. They were two very different personalities, but they had all these qualities in common, and after so many years they are still lovable.

At the corner of Bolton Street is 81 Piccadilly, once a reckless gambling club, with splendid food, where handsome Beau Brummell was president. He was the grandson of a "gentleman's gentleman" who let lodgings in Bury Street, but he went to Eton and was the best scholar, wet-bob and cricketer of his time. He set himself to become the intimate of people in high society, and even if it was a foolish ambition it could not have been achieved and maintained by a fool. "The man was no fool," wrote strong-minded Lady Hester Stanhope, and "I should like to see him again." Sheridan, William Lamb, Georgiana Duchess of Devonshire and Byron were among those who wrote verses in his album. He too could write verses, draw, dance beautifully. He was excellent company, amusing, adroit and really gay. As an arbiter of fashion he chose elegant simplicity and clean linen. He quarrelled with his patron and admirer the Prince Regent in 1813; and when, with Lord Alvanley, he ran into the Regent, who spoke to his companion but cut him dead, he valiantly interrupted to ask Alvanley, "Who's your fat friend?" Utterly ruined by gambling, he fled three years later to Calais, and Charles Greville wrote of him there in 1830 with charming shabby furniture and a great green macaw, "full of gaiety, impudence and misery." In his ten remaining years he sank to the debtor's prison at Caen, to madness, and to death in the pauper lunatic asylum.

In early 1801, soon after their return from Naples, Sir William and Lady Hamilton settled at 23 Piccadilly, a little house between the Savile Club and Down Street. Nelson lodged in St James's Street. Sir William was a contented cuckold and carried the position well; he had sympathy and admiration for the lovers, they liked and respected him. Nelson was soon off to sea again, writing those lamentably jealous letters, but No 23 had plenty of visitors, though Lady Hamilton was not quite "in society." Georgiana Duchess of Devonshire, who had a softness for her beauty, came, of course, with her delightful cousin Diana Beauclerk; and there was Old Q., the Duke of Queensberry, who remembered Lady Hamilton in his will; and Italian refugees and the Kembles and so on. On one occasion Lady Hamilton danced a tarantella, a sort of nymph-and-satyr dance and remarkably hot stuff, with such merry vigour that she wore out four partners—her elderly husband, the forty years younger Duke of Noria, her maid-servant and a perfectly black Copt woman given her by Nelson. At least one spectator was especially struck by the gay agility of Sir William Hamilton.

And so we come to No. 1, London, Apsley House at Hyde Park Corner, where lived the Duke of Wellington. In 1831 his wife lay dying there, and the mob came up and stoned his windows, destroying pictures within, because he opposed Parliamentary reform. Upon this he ordered the famous iron shutters. Twelve years later when a great cheering crowd followed him up Constitution Hill he trotted quietly along ignoring them till he reached his gates; then he pointed at those iron shutters and rode silently in.

He was a fine-looking man, with large dark-blue eyes more dominating than his aquiline nose, and Keeper Jones of the Royal Academy was proud to be often taken for him. "Strange," said the Duke, when told of it. "No one ever takes me for Mr Jones." However, someone did say to him, "Mr Smith, I believe?" He replied, "Sir, if you believe that, you would believe anything."

The Duke was noted for his *sang froid* in times of stress. "Publish and be damned," he said to the blackmailer. When he was in great danger of being drowned at sea, and the Captain of the vessel came to him at bedtime exclaiming, "It will soon be all over with us," he replied after a second's consideration, "Very well, then I shall not take off my boots." He expected similar self-command in others, and once when he found a little boy crying and the explanation began with the fact that he had to go away to school next morning, the Duke was severe upon his lack of fortitude. But he was a just man, and when the lad had further explained that he did not fear school but wept to leave a favourite toad among indifferent people without hope of getting news of it, he apologized. In due course the boy received a letter:

"F.M. the Duke of Wellington presents his compliments to Master Blank and begs to inform him that his toad is well." He could take genuine emotion, but not sentimental tosh, and when a stranger who had rendered him some small service and been properly thanked burst into a rhapsody about this being the happiest, proudest moment of his life, the Duke felt constrained to advise him, "Don't be a damned fool, sir."

He was interesting, as was natural, about Waterloo: "The nearest run thing you ever saw in your life. . . . By God! I don't think it would have done if I had not been there." He said too, "I have found that raw troops, however inferior to the old ones in manœuvring, are far superior to them in downright hard fighting with the enemy; at Waterloo, the young ensigns and lieutenants, who had never before seen a battle, rushed to meet death as if they had been playing cricket."

This awe-inspiring man—for he did inspire awe—was very susceptible as everyone knows, much talked of with women, much taken up and tyrannized with their gossip and little affairs, ever ready for charades and romps with the ladies at house parties. "I suppose, Duke," a woman once said to him, "you have inspired a great deal of admiration and enthusiasm among women during your life?" He answered, "Oh, yes, plenty of that! plenty of that! But no woman ever loved me: never in my whole life."

With his greatness and his iron shutters and his deprivation of love, he is an immortal ghost of London indeed.

There they are: all valiant dust that builds on dust; the third little pig, who built his house of bricks; the golden lads and girls, all lovers young and even the chimney-sweepers; withered murder, Tarquin's ravishing strides; the beasts, that are also of His household; as on a darkling plain swept with confused alarms of struggle and flight—and even the good shall hardly be safe, poor things. Go, lovely rose, tell—tell—the grave's a fine and private place; they took their wages, and are dead. But it was not unknown to be merry and wise, happy and good. None of these strangers and sojourners was always a-weary of the sun.

Bibliography

Old & New London. Thornbury & Walford
Famous Houses & Literary Shrines of London. St. John Adcock
London for the Literary Pilgrim. William Kent
Six Criminal Women. Elizabeth Jenkins
Theatre Royal, Drury Lane. W. J. Macqueen Pope
Twelve Bad Men. Edited by Thomas Seccombe
Twelve Bad Women. Edited by Arthur Vincent
The Grand Whiggery. Marjorie Villiers
Table-Talk. Samuel Rogers
A mid-Victorian Pepys. Edited by Ellis
London in the Sixties. By one of the Old Brigade
Ghosts of Piccadilly. G. S. Street
The Pre-Raphaelite Tragedy. William Gaunt
The Queens of Society. Grace & Philip Wharton
Some Human Oddities. Eric John Dingwall
Famous Trials—I. Edited by Harry Hodge (Penguin Books)
Famous Trials—II. Edited by Harry Hodge (Penguin Books)
The Trial of Oscar Wilde. Edited by H. Montgomery Hyde. Notable British Trials Series No. 70
Leigh Hunt. Edmund Blunden
Keats. Betty Askwith
London, or Interesting Memorials of its Rise, Progress and Present State. Sholte & Reuben Percy, Brothers of the Benedictine Monastery
A Life of William Shakespeare. Sir Sidney Lee
The Showman of Vanity Fair. Lionel Stevenson

Index